T0354562

BIBLE JOURNAL
NOTEBOOK

<u>Genesis - Revelation</u>
Study, Take Notes & Research
The Scriptures to
Show Thyself Approved
Unto God

²Tim 2:15

DARCELL LEMMONS

Order this book online at www.trafford.com
or email orders@trafford.com

Most Trafford titles are also available at major online book retailers.

All Scripture Reference were taken from
The Old and New Testament, KJV
by Thomas Nelson, Inc.
Camden, New Jersey 08103
By Permission.

Proofread by: R. Cunningham

Cover Design By: D. Wright

Printed in the United States of America.

ISBN: 978-1-4669-9536-9 (sc)
ISBN: 978-1-4669-9535-2 (e)

Trafford rev. 07/02/2013

 www.trafford.com

North America & International
toll-free: 1 888 232 4444 (USA & Canada)
fax: 812 355 4082

Dedication

This Bible Journal Notebook is dedicated to the Ministers of God, the Sunday School Teachers, and to the Bible Students. Keep track of your personal study notes, comments, thoughts, and revelation of God's Holy Word.

The Old Testament

Scripture Notes

> ***Study to show thyself approved unto God,***
> ***A workman that needeth not be ashamed***
> ***rightly dividing the word of truth.***
> *²Tim 2:15*

Date:

Speaker:

Sermon Title:

Scripture Notes

Personal Revelation:

Appointments:

Tithe/Offering:

GENESIS

> *Study to show thyself approved unto God,*
> *A workman that needeth not be ashamed*
> *rightly dividing the word of truth.*
> *²Tim 2:15*

Date:

Speaker:

Sermon Title:

Scripture Notes

Personal Revelation:

Appointments:

Tithe/Offering:

GENESIS

> ***Study to show thyself approved unto God,***
> ***A workman that needeth not be ashamed***
> ***rightly dividing the word of truth.***
> *²Tim 2:15*

Date:
Speaker:
Sermon Title:

Scripture Notes

Personal Revelation:

Appointments:

Tithe/Offering:

GENESIS

> *Study to show thyself approved unto God,*
> *A workman that needeth not be ashamed*
> *rightly dividing the word of truth.*
> *²Tim 2:15*

Date:

Speaker:

Sermon Title:

Scripture Notes

Personal Revelation:

Appointments:

Tithe/Offering:

GENESIS

Study to show thyself approved unto God,
A workman that needeth not be ashamed
rightly dividing the word of truth.
²Tim 2:15

Date:
Speaker:
Sermon Title:

Scripture Notes

GENESIS

Personal Revelation:

Appointments:

Tithe/Offering:

> *Study to show thyself approved unto God,*
> *A workman that needeth not be ashamed*
> *rightly dividing the word of truth.*
> *²Tim 2:15*

Date:

Speaker:

Sermon Title:

Scripture Notes

GENESIS

Personal Revelation:

Appointments:

Tithe/Offering:

Study to show thyself approved unto God,
A workman that needeth not be ashamed
rightly dividing the word of truth.
²Tim 2:15

Date:

Speaker:

Sermon Title:

Scripture Notes

GENESIS

Personal Revelation:

Appointments:

Tithe/Offering:

Study to show thyself approved unto God, A workman that needeth not be ashamed rightly dividing the word of truth. *²Tim 2:15*	

Date:
Speaker:
Sermon Title:

Scripture Notes

EXODUS

Personal Revelation:

Appointments:

Tithe/Offering:

Study to show thyself approved unto God,
A workman that needeth not be ashamed
rightly dividing the word of truth.
²Tim 2:15

Date:
Speaker:
Sermon Title:

Scripture Notes

EXODUS

Personal Revelation:

Appointments:

Tithe/Offering:

Study to show thyself approved unto God,
A workman that needeth not be ashamed
rightly dividing the word of truth.
²Tim 2:15

Date:
Speaker:
Sermon Title:

Scripture Notes

Personal Revelation:

Appointments:

Tithe/Offering:

EXODUS

Study to show thyself approved unto God,
A workman that needeth not be ashamed
rightly dividing the word of truth.
²Tim 2:15

Date:
Speaker:
Sermon Title:

Scripture Notes

EXODUS

Personal Revelation:

Appointments:

Tithe/Offering:

Study to show thyself approved unto God,
A workman that needeth not be ashamed
rightly dividing the word of truth.
²Tim 2:15

Date:
Speaker:
Sermon Title:

Scripture Notes

Personal Revelation:

Appointments:

Tithe/Offering:

EXODUS

Study to show thyself approved unto God,
A workman that needeth not be ashamed
rightly dividing the word of truth.
²Tim 2:15

Date:
Speaker:
Sermon Title:

Scripture Notes

EXODUS

Personal Revelation:

Appointments:

Tithe/Offering:

Study to show thyself approved unto God,
A workman that needeth not be ashamed
rightly dividing the word of truth.
²Tim 2:15

Date:
Speaker:
Sermon Title:

Scripture Notes

EXODUS

Personal Revelation:

Appointments:

Tithe/Offering:

Study to show thyself approved unto God, *A workman that needeth not be ashamed* *rightly dividing the word of truth.* *²Tim 2:15*

Date:

Speaker:

Sermon Title:

Scripture Notes

LEVITICUS

Personal Revelation:

Appointments:

Tithe/Offering:

Study to show thyself approved unto God,
A workman that needeth not be ashamed
rightly dividing the word of truth.
²Tim 2:15

Date:
Speaker:
Sermon Title:

Scripture Notes

Personal Revelation:

Appointments:

Tithe/Offering:

LEVITICUS

Study to show thyself approved unto God,
A workman that needeth not be ashamed
rightly dividing the word of truth.
²Tim 2:15

Date:
Speaker:
Sermon Title:

Scripture Notes

LEVITICUS

Personal Revelation:

Appointments:

Tithe/Offering:

Study to show thyself approved unto God,
A workman that needeth not be ashamed
rightly dividing the word of truth.
²Tim 2:15

Date:
Speaker:
Sermon Title:

Scripture Notes

Personal Revelation:

Appointments:

Tithe/Offering:

LEVITICUS

Study to show thyself approved unto God,
A workman that needeth not be ashamed
rightly dividing the word of truth.
²Tim 2:15

Date:
Speaker:
Sermon Title:

Scripture Notes

LEVITICUS

Personal Revelation:

Appointments:

Tithe/Offering:

Study to show thyself approved unto God,
A workman that needeth not be ashamed
rightly dividing the word of truth.
²Tim 2:15

Date:
Speaker:
Sermon Title:

Scripture Notes

Personal Revelation:

Appointments:

Tithe/Offering:

LEVITICUS

Study to show thyself approved unto God,
A workman that needeth not be ashamed
rightly dividing the word of truth.
²Tim 2:15

Date:
Speaker:
Sermon Title:

Scripture Notes

LEVITICUS

Personal Revelation:

Appointments:

Tithe/Offering:

Study to show thyself approved unto God,
A workman that needeth not be ashamed
rightly dividing the word of truth.
²Tim 2:15

Date:
Speaker:
Sermon Title:

Scripture Notes

Personal Revelation:

Appointments:

Tithe/Offering:

NUMBERS

Study to show thyself approved unto God,
A workman that needeth not be ashamed
rightly dividing the word of truth.
²Tim 2:15

Date:
Speaker:
Sermon Title:

Scripture Notes

Personal Revelation:

Appointments:

Tithe/Offering:

NUMBERS

Study to show thyself approved unto God,
A workman that needeth not be ashamed
rightly dividing the word of truth.
²Tim 2:15

Date:

Speaker:

Sermon Title:

Scripture Notes

Personal Revelation:

Appointments:

Tithe/Offering:

NUMBERS

Study to show thyself approved unto God,
A workman that needeth not be ashamed
rightly dividing the word of truth.
²Tim 2:15

Date:
Speaker:
Sermon Title:

Scripture Notes

Personal Revelation:

Appointments:

Tithe/Offering:

NUMBERS

Study to show thyself approved unto God,
A workman that needeth not be ashamed
rightly dividing the word of truth.
²Tim 2:15

Date:

Speaker:

Sermon Title:

Scripture Notes

Personal Revelation:

Appointments:

Tithe/Offering:

NUMBERS

Study to show thyself approved unto God,
A workman that needeth not be ashamed
rightly dividing the word of truth.
²Tim 2:15

Date:
Speaker:
Sermon Title:

Scripture Notes

Personal Revelation:

Appointments:

Tithe/Offering:

NUMBERS

Study to show thyself approved unto God,
A workman that needeth not be ashamed
rightly dividing the word of truth.
²Tim 2:15

Date:
Speaker:
Sermon Title:

Scripture Notes

Personal Revelation:

Appointments:

Tithe/Offering:

NUMBERS

*Study to show thyself approved unto God,
A workman that needeth not be ashamed
rightly dividing the word of truth.*
2Tim 2:15

Date:
Speaker:
Sermon Title:

Scripture Notes

DEUTERONOMY

Personal Revelation:

Appointments:

Tithe/Offering:

Study to show thyself approved unto God, *A workman that needeth not be ashamed* *rightly dividing the word of truth.* *²Tim 2:15*	
Date: **Speaker:** **Sermon Title:**	
Scripture Notes	
Personal Revelation:	
Appointments:	
Tithe/Offering:	

DEUTERONOMY

Study to show thyself approved unto God,
A workman that needeth not be ashamed
rightly dividing the word of truth.
²Tim 2:15

Date:
Speaker:
Sermon Title:

Scripture Notes

Personal Revelation:

Appointments:

Tithe/Offering:

DEUTERONOMY

Study to show thyself approved unto God,
A workman that needeth not be ashamed
rightly dividing the word of truth.
²Tim 2:15

Date:
Speaker:
Sermon Title:

Scripture Notes

Personal Revelation:

Appointments:

Tithe/Offering:

DEUTERONOMY

Study to show thyself approved unto God,
A workman that needeth not be ashamed
rightly dividing the word of truth.
²Tim 2:15

Date:
Speaker:
Sermon Title:

Scripture Notes

Personal Revelation:

Appointments:

Tithe/Offering:

DEUTERONOMY

Study to show thyself approved unto God,
A workman that needeth not be ashamed
rightly dividing the word of truth.
²Tim 2:15

Date:

Speaker:

Sermon Title:

Scripture Notes

DEUTERONOMY

Personal Revelation:

Appointments:

Tithe/Offering:

> *Study to show thyself approved unto God,*
> *A workman that needeth not be ashamed*
> *rightly dividing the word of truth.*
> *²Tim 2:15*

Date:

Speaker:

Sermon Title:

Scripture Notes

_____
_____
_____
_____
_____
_____
_____
_____
_____
_____
_____
_____
_____
_____
_____
_____
_____
_____
_____
_____
_____
_____

Personal Revelation:

Appointments:

Tithe/Offering:

DEUTERONOMY

Study to show thyself approved unto God,
A workman that needeth not be ashamed
rightly dividing the word of truth.
²Tim 2:15

Date:
Speaker:
Sermon Title:

Scripture Notes

JOSHUA

Personal Revelation:

Appointments:

Tithe/Offering:

Study to show thyself approved unto God,
A workman that needeth not be ashamed
rightly dividing the word of truth.
²Tim 2:15

Date:
Speaker:
Sermon Title:

Scripture Notes

Personal Revelation:

Appointments:

Tithe/Offering:

JOSHUA

Study to show thyself approved unto God,
A workman that needeth not be ashamed
rightly dividing the word of truth.
²Tim 2:15

Date:
Speaker:
Sermon Title:

Scripture Notes

JOSHUA

Personal Revelation:

Appointments:

Tithe/Offering:

Study to show thyself approved unto God,
A workman that needeth not be ashamed
rightly dividing the word of truth.
²Tim 2:15

Date:
Speaker:
Sermon Title:

Scripture Notes

JOSHUA

Personal Revelation:

Appointments:

Tithe/Offering:

Study to show thyself approved unto God,
A workman that needeth not be ashamed
rightly dividing the word of truth.
²Tim 2:15

Date:
Speaker:
Sermon Title:

Scripture Notes

JOSHUA

Personal Revelation:

Appointments:

Tithe/Offering:

Study to show thyself approved unto God,
A workman that needeth not be ashamed
rightly dividing the word of truth.
²Tim 2:15

Date:
Speaker:
Sermon Title:

Scripture Notes

JOSHUA

Personal Revelation:

Appointments:

Tithe/Offering:

Study to show thyself approved unto God,
A workman that needeth not be ashamed
rightly dividing the word of truth.
²Tim 2:15

Date:
Speaker:
Sermon Title:

Scripture Notes

JOSHUA

Personal Revelation:

Appointments:

Tithe/Offering:

Study to show thyself approved unto God,
A workman that needeth not be ashamed
rightly dividing the word of truth.
²Tim 2:15

Date:
Speaker:
Sermon Title:

Scripture Notes

Personal Revelation:

Appointments:

Tithe/Offering:

JUDGES

Study to show thyself approved unto God,
A workman that needeth not be ashamed
rightly dividing the word of truth.
²Tim 2:15

Date:
Speaker:
Sermon Title:

Scripture Notes

Personal Revelation:

Appointments:

Tithe/Offering:

JUDGES

Study to show thyself approved unto God,
A workman that needeth not be ashamed
rightly dividing the word of truth.
²Tim 2:15

Date:
Speaker:
Sermon Title:

Scripture Notes

JUDGES

Personal Revelation:

Appointments:

Tithe/Offering:

Study to show thyself approved unto God,
A workman that needeth not be ashamed
rightly dividing the word of truth.
²Tim 2:15

Date:
Speaker:
Sermon Title:

Scripture Notes

Personal Revelation:

Appointments:

Tithe/Offering:

JUDGES

Study to show thyself approved unto God,
A workman that needeth not be ashamed
rightly dividing the word of truth.
²Tim 2:15

Date:
Speaker:
Sermon Title:

Scripture Notes

JUDGES

Personal Revelation:

Appointments:

Tithe/Offering:

> *Study to show thyself approved unto God,*
> *A workman that needeth not be ashamed*
> *rightly dividing the word of truth.*
> *²Tim 2:15*

Date:
Speaker:
Sermon Title:

Scripture Notes

Personal Revelation:

Appointments:

Tithe/Offering:

JUDGES

Study to show thyself approved unto God,
A workman that needeth not be ashamed
rightly dividing the word of truth.
²Tim 2:15

Date:
Speaker:
Sermon Title:

Scripture Notes

Personal Revelation:

Appointments:

Tithe/Offering:

JUDGES

Study to show thyself approved unto God,
A workman that needeth not be ashamed
rightly dividing the word of truth.
²Tim 2:15

Date:
Speaker:
Sermon Title:

Scripture Notes

RUTH

Personal Revelation:

Appointments:

Tithe/Offering:

Study to show thyself approved unto God,
A workman that needeth not be ashamed
rightly dividing the word of truth.
²Tim 2:15

Date:
Speaker:
Sermon Title:

Scripture Notes

Personal Revelation:

Appointments:

Tithe/Offering:

RUTH

> *Study to show thyself approved unto God,*
> *A workman that needeth not be ashamed*
> *rightly dividing the word of truth.*
> *²Tim 2:15*

Date:
Speaker:
Sermon Title:

Scripture Notes

Personal Revelation:

Appointments:

Tithe/Offering:

RUTH

Study to show thyself approved unto God,
A workman that needeth not be ashamed
rightly dividing the word of truth.
²Tim 2:15

Date:
Speaker:
Sermon Title:

Scripture Notes

Personal Revelation:

Appointments:

Tithe/Offering:

RUTH

> *Study to show thyself approved unto God,*
> *A workman that needeth not be ashamed*
> *rightly dividing the word of truth.*
> *²Tim 2:15*

Date:
Speaker:
Sermon Title:

Scripture Notes

Personal Revelation:

Appointments:

Tithe/Offering:

RUTH

Study to show thyself approved unto God,
A workman that needeth not be ashamed
rightly dividing the word of truth.
²Tim 2:15

Date:
Speaker:
Sermon Title:

Scripture Notes

Personal Revelation:

Appointments:

Tithe/Offering:

RUTH

Study to show thyself approved unto God,
A workman that needeth not be ashamed
rightly dividing the word of truth.
²Tim 2:15

Date:

Speaker:

Sermon Title:

Scripture Notes

Personal Revelation:

Appointments:

Tithe/Offering:

RUTH

Study to show thyself approved unto God, A workman that needeth not be ashamed rightly dividing the word of truth. *²Tim 2:15*

Date:

Speaker:

Sermon Title:

Scripture Notes

1SAMUEL

Personal Revelation:

Appointments:

Tithe/Offering:

Study to show thyself approved unto God,
A workman that needeth not be ashamed
rightly dividing the word of truth.
²Tim 2:15

Date:
Speaker:
Sermon Title:

Scripture Notes

Personal Revelation:

Appointments:

Tithe/Offering:

1SAMUEL

Study to show thyself approved unto God,
A workman that needeth not be ashamed
rightly dividing the word of truth.
²Tim 2:15

Date:
Speaker:
Sermon Title:

Scripture Notes

1SAMUEL

Personal Revelation:

Appointments:

Tithe/Offering:

Study to show thyself approved unto God,
A workman that needeth not be ashamed
rightly dividing the word of truth.
²Tim 2:15

Date:

Speaker:

Sermon Title:

Scripture Notes

Personal Revelation:

Appointments:

Tithe/Offering:

1SAMUEL

Study to show thyself approved unto God,
A workman that needeth not be ashamed
rightly dividing the word of truth.
²Tim 2:15

Date:
Speaker:
Sermon Title:

Scripture Notes

Personal Revelation:

Appointments:

Tithe/Offering:

1SAMUEL

Study to show thyself approved unto God,
A workman that needeth not be ashamed
rightly dividing the word of truth.
²Tim 2:15

Date:
Speaker:
Sermon Title:

Scripture Notes

Personal Revelation:

Appointments:

Tithe/Offering:

1SAMUEL

Study to show thyself approved unto God, A workman that needeth not be ashamed rightly dividing the word of truth. *²Tim 2:15*	
Date: **Speaker:** **Sermon Title:**	
Scripture Notes	
	¹SAMUEL
Personal Revelation:	
Appointments:	
Tithe/Offering:	

Study to show thyself approved unto God,
A workman that needeth not be ashamed
rightly dividing the word of truth.
²Tim 2:15

Date:
Speaker:
Sermon Title:

Scripture Notes

Personal Revelation:

Appointments:

Tithe/Offering:

²SAMUEL

Study to show thyself approved unto God,
A workman that needeth not be ashamed
rightly dividing the word of truth.
²Tim 2:15

Date:
Speaker:
Sermon Title:

Scripture Notes

Personal Revelation:

Appointments:

Tithe/Offering:

2 SAMUEL

Study to show thyself approved unto God,
A workman that needeth not be ashamed
rightly dividing the word of truth.
²Tim 2:15

Date:

Speaker:

Sermon Title:

Scripture Notes

Personal Revelation:

Appointments:

Tithe/Offering:

²SAMUEL

Study to show thyself approved unto God,
A workman that needeth not be ashamed
rightly dividing the word of truth.
²Tim 2:15

Date:
Speaker:
Sermon Title:

Scripture Notes

2 SAMUEL

Personal Revelation:

Appointments:

Tithe/Offering:

*Study to show thyself approved unto God,
A workman that needeth not be ashamed
rightly dividing the word of truth.*
²Tim 2:15

Date:
Speaker:
Sermon Title:

Scripture Notes

Personal Revelation:

Appointments:

Tithe/Offering:

²SAMUEL

Study to show thyself approved unto God,
A workman that needeth not be ashamed
rightly dividing the word of truth.
²Tim 2:15

Date:
Speaker:
Sermon Title:

Scripture Notes

Personal Revelation:

Appointments:

Tithe/Offering:

²SAMUEL

Darcell Lemmons

Study to show thyself approved unto God,
A workman that needeth not be ashamed
rightly dividing the word of truth.
²Tim 2:15

Date:
Speaker:
Sermon Title:

Scripture Notes

²SAMUEL

Personal Revelation:

Appointments:

Tithe/Offering:

Study to show thyself approved unto God,
A workman that needeth not be ashamed
rightly dividing the word of truth.
²Tim 2:15

Date:
Speaker:
Sermon Title:

Scripture Notes

Personal Revelation:

Appointments:

Tithe/Offering:

1KINGS

Study to show thyself approved unto God,
A workman that needeth not be ashamed
rightly dividing the word of truth.
²Tim 2:15

Date:

Speaker:

Sermon Title:

Scripture Notes

Personal Revelation:

Appointments:

Tithe/Offering:

¹KINGS

Study to show thyself approved unto God,
A workman that needeth not be ashamed
rightly dividing the word of truth.
²Tim 2:15

Date:

Speaker:

Sermon Title:

Scripture Notes

Personal Revelation:

Appointments:

Tithe/Offering:

¹KINGS

Study to show thyself approved unto God,
A workman that needeth not be ashamed
rightly dividing the word of truth.
²Tim 2:15

Date:
Speaker:
Sermon Title:

Scripture Notes

1KINGS

Personal Revelation:

Appointments:

Tithe/Offering:

Study to show thyself approved unto God,
A workman that needeth not be ashamed
rightly dividing the word of truth.
²Tim 2:15

Date:
Speaker:
Sermon Title:

Scripture Notes

Personal Revelation:

Appointments:

Tithe/Offering:

1KINGS

Study to show thyself approved unto God,
A workman that needeth not be ashamed
rightly dividing the word of truth.
²Tim 2:15

Date:
Speaker:
Sermon Title:

Scripture Notes

Personal Revelation:

Appointments:

Tithe/Offering:

1KINGS

Study to show thyself approved unto God,
A workman that needeth not be ashamed
rightly dividing the word of truth.
²Tim 2:15

Date:
Speaker:
Sermon Title:

Scripture Notes

Personal Revelation:

Appointments:

Tithe/Offering:

1KINGS

Study to show thyself approved unto God,
A workman that needeth not be ashamed
rightly dividing the word of truth.
²Tim 2:15

Date:
Speaker:
Sermon Title:

Scripture Notes

Personal Revelation:

Appointments:

Tithe/Offering:

²KINGS

Study to show thyself approved unto God,
A workman that needeth not be ashamed
rightly dividing the word of truth.
²Tim 2:15

Date:
Speaker:
Sermon Title:

Scripture Notes

Personal Revelation:

Appointments:

Tithe/Offering:

²KINGS

Study to show thyself approved unto God,
A workman that needeth not be ashamed
rightly dividing the word of truth.
²Tim 2:15

Date:
Speaker:
Sermon Title:

Scripture Notes

Personal Revelation:

Appointments:

Tithe/Offering:

²KINGS

Study to show thyself approved unto God,
A workman that needeth not be ashamed
rightly dividing the word of truth.
²Tim 2:15

Date:
Speaker:
Sermon Title:

Scripture Notes

Personal Revelation:

Appointments:

Tithe/Offering:

2KINGS

Study to show thyself approved unto God,
A workman that needeth not be ashamed
rightly dividing the word of truth.
²Tim 2:15

Date:
Speaker:
Sermon Title:

Scripture Notes

²KINGS

Personal Revelation:

Appointments:

Tithe/Offering:

Study to show thyself approved unto God,
A workman that needeth not be ashamed
rightly dividing the word of truth.
²Tim 2:15

Date:

Speaker:

Sermon Title:

Scripture Notes

Personal Revelation:

Appointments:

Tithe/Offering:

²KINGS

Study to show thyself approved unto God,
A workman that needeth not be ashamed
rightly dividing the word of truth.
²Tim 2:15

Date:
Speaker:
Sermon Title:

Scripture Notes

2KINGS

Personal Revelation:

Appointments:

Tithe/Offering:

Study to show thyself approved unto God,
A workman that needeth not be ashamed
rightly dividing the word of truth.
²Tim 2:15

Date:
Speaker:
Sermon Title:

Scripture Notes

1 CHRONICLES

Personal Revelation:

Appointments:

Tithe/Offering:

Study to show thyself approved unto God,
A workman that needeth not be ashamed
rightly dividing the word of truth.
²Tim 2:15

Date:

Speaker:

Sermon Title:

Scripture Notes

Personal Revelation:

Appointments:

Tithe/Offering:

¹CHRONICLES

Study to show thyself approved unto God,
A workman that needeth not be ashamed
rightly dividing the word of truth.
²Tim 2:15

Date:
Speaker:
Sermon Title:

Scripture Notes

1CHRONICLES

Personal Revelation:

Appointments:

Tithe/Offering:

Study to show thyself approved unto God,
A workman that needeth not be ashamed
rightly dividing the word of truth.
²Tim 2:15

Date:
Speaker:
Sermon Title:

Scripture Notes

Personal Revelation:

Appointments:

Tithe/Offering:

¹CHRONICLES

Study to show thyself approved unto God,
A workman that needeth not be ashamed
rightly dividing the word of truth.
²Tim 2:15

Date:
Speaker:
Sermon Title:

Scripture Notes

1CHRONICLES

Personal Revelation:

Appointments:

Tithe/Offering:

Study to show thyself approved unto God,
A workman that needeth not be ashamed
rightly dividing the word of truth.
²Tim 2:15

Date:
Speaker:
Sermon Title:

Scripture Notes

Personal Revelation:

Appointments:

Tithe/Offering:

¹CHRONICLES

Study to show thyself approved unto God,
A workman that needeth not be ashamed
rightly dividing the word of truth.
²Tim 2:15

Date:
Speaker:
Sermon Title:

Scripture Notes

Personal Revelation:

Appointments:

Tithe/Offering:

1CHRONICLES

Study to show thyself approved unto God,
A workman that needeth not be ashamed
rightly dividing the word of truth.
²Tim 2:15

Date:
Speaker:
Sermon Title:

Scripture Notes

²CHRONICLES

Personal Revelation:

Appointments:

Tithe/Offering:

Study to show thyself approved unto God,
A workman that needeth not be ashamed
rightly dividing the word of truth.
²Tim 2:15

Date:
Speaker:
Sermon Title:

Scripture Notes

Personal Revelation:

Appointments:

Tithe/Offering:

2CHRONICLES

Study to show thyself approved unto God,
A workman that needeth not be ashamed
rightly dividing the word of truth.
²Tim 2:15

Date:

Speaker:

Sermon Title:

Scripture Notes

2CHRONICLES

Personal Revelation:

Appointments:

Tithe/Offering:

Study to show thyself approved unto God,
A workman that needeth not be ashamed
rightly dividing the word of truth.
²Tim 2:15

Date:
Speaker:
Sermon Title:

Scripture Notes

2CHRONICLES

Personal Revelation:

Appointments:

Tithe/Offering:

Study to show thyself approved unto God,
A workman that needeth not be ashamed
rightly dividing the word of truth.
²Tim 2:15

Date:

Speaker:

Sermon Title:

Scripture Notes

2CHRONICLES

Personal Revelation:

Appointments:

Tithe/Offering:

Study to show thyself approved unto God,
A workman that needeth not be ashamed
rightly dividing the word of truth.
²Tim 2:15

Date:
Speaker:
Sermon Title:

Scripture Notes

Personal Revelation:

Appointments:

Tithe/Offering:

²CHRONICLES

Study to show thyself approved unto God,
A workman that needeth not be ashamed
rightly dividing the word of truth.
²Tim 2:15

Date:
Speaker:
Sermon Title:

Scripture Notes

2CHRONICLES

Personal Revelation:

Appointments:

Tithe/Offering:

Study to show thyself approved unto God,
A workman that needeth not be ashamed
rightly dividing the word of truth.
²Tim 2:15

Date:
Speaker:
Sermon Title:

Scripture Notes

EZRA

Personal Revelation:

Appointments:

Tithe/Offering:

> *Study to show thyself approved unto God,*
> *A workman that needeth not be ashamed*
> *rightly dividing the word of truth.*
> *²Tim 2:15*

Date:

Speaker:

Sermon Title:

Scripture Notes

EZRA

Personal Revelation:

Appointments:

Tithe/Offering:

> *Study to show thyself approved unto God,*
> *A workman that needeth not be ashamed*
> *rightly dividing the word of truth.*
> *²Tim 2:15*

Date:

Speaker:

Sermon Title:

Scripture Notes

EZRA

Personal Revelation:

Appointments:

Tithe/Offering:

> *Study to show thyself approved unto God,*
> *A workman that needeth not be ashamed*
> *rightly dividing the word of truth.*
> *²Tim 2:15*

Date:
Speaker:
Sermon Title:

Scripture Notes

EZRA

Personal Revelation:

Appointments:

Tithe/Offering:

Study to show thyself approved unto God,
A workman that needeth not be ashamed
rightly dividing the word of truth.
²Tim 2:15

Date:
Speaker:
Sermon Title:

Scripture Notes

EZRA

Personal Revelation:

Appointments:

Tithe/Offering:

> *Study to show thyself approved unto God,*
> *A workman that needeth not be ashamed*
> *rightly dividing the word of truth.*
> *²Tim 2:15*

Date:

Speaker:

Sermon Title:

Scripture Notes

Personal Revelation:

Appointments:

Tithe/Offering:

EZRA

Study to show thyself approved unto God, A workman that needeth not be ashamed rightly dividing the word of truth. ²Tim 2:15

Date:
Speaker:
Sermon Title:

Scripture Notes

EZRA

Personal Revelation:

Appointments:

Tithe/Offering:

Study to show thyself approved unto God,
A workman that needeth not be ashamed
rightly dividing the word of truth.
²Tim 2:15

Date:
Speaker:
Sermon Title:

Scripture Notes

Personal Revelation:

Appointments:

Tithe/Offering:

NEHEMIAH

Study to show thyself approved unto God,
A workman that needeth not be ashamed
rightly dividing the word of truth.
²Tim 2:15

Date:
Speaker:
Sermon Title:

Scripture Notes

NEHEMIAH

Personal Revelation:

Appointments:

Tithe/Offering:

Study to show thyself approved unto God,
A workman that needeth not be ashamed
rightly dividing the word of truth.
²Tim 2:15

Date:
Speaker:
Sermon Title:

Scripture Notes

Personal Revelation:

Appointments:

Tithe/Offering:

NEHEMIAH

Study to show thyself approved unto God,
A workman that needeth not be ashamed
rightly dividing the word of truth.
²Tim 2:15

Date:
Speaker:
Sermon Title:

Scripture Notes

NEHEMIAH

Personal Revelation:

Appointments:

Tithe/Offering:

Study to show thyself approved unto God,
A workman that needeth not be ashamed
rightly dividing the word of truth.
²Tim 2:15

Date:

Speaker:

Sermon Title:

Scripture Notes

NEHEMIAH

Personal Revelation:

Appointments:

Tithe/Offering:

Study to show thyself approved unto God,
A workman that needeth not be ashamed
rightly dividing the word of truth.
²Tim 2:15

Date:
Speaker:
Sermon Title:

Scripture Notes

NEHEMIAH

Personal Revelation:

Appointments:

Tithe/Offering:

***Study to show thyself approved unto God,
A workman that needeth not be ashamed
rightly dividing the word of truth.***
²Tim 2:15

Date:
Speaker:
Sermon Title:

Scripture Notes

NEHEMIAH

Personal Revelation:

Appointments:

Tithe/Offering:

Study to show thyself approved unto God,
A workman that needeth not be ashamed
rightly dividing the word of truth.
²Tim 2:15

Date:

Speaker:

Sermon Title:

Scripture Notes

Personal Revelation:

Appointments:

Tithe/Offering:

ESTHER

Study to show thyself approved unto God,
A workman that needeth not be ashamed
rightly dividing the word of truth.
²Tim 2:15

Date:

Speaker:

Sermon Title:

Scripture Notes

Personal Revelation:

Appointments:

Tithe/Offering:

ESTHER

Study to show thyself approved unto God,
A workman that needeth not be ashamed
rightly dividing the word of truth.
²Tim 2:15

Date:
Speaker:
Sermon Title:

Scripture Notes

ESTHER

Personal Revelation:

Appointments:

Tithe/Offering:

Study to show thyself approved unto God,
A workman that needeth not be ashamed
rightly dividing the word of truth.
²Tim 2:15

Date:
Speaker:
Sermon Title:

Scripture Notes

ESTHER

Personal Revelation:

Appointments:

Tithe/Offering:

Study to show thyself approved unto God,
A workman that needeth not be ashamed
rightly dividing the word of truth.
²Tim 2:15

Date:
Speaker:
Sermon Title:

Scripture Notes

Personal Revelation:

Appointments:

Tithe/Offering:

ESTHER

Study to show thyself approved unto God, A workman that needeth not be ashamed rightly dividing the word of truth.   *²Tim 2:15*

Date:
Speaker:
Sermon Title:

Scripture Notes

ESTHER

Personal Revelation:

Appointments:

Tithe/Offering:

Study to show thyself approved unto God,
A workman that needeth not be ashamed
rightly dividing the word of truth.
²Tim 2:15

Date:
Speaker:
Sermon Title:

Scripture Notes

ESTHER

Personal Revelation:

Appointments:

Tithe/Offering:

Study to show thyself approved unto God,
A workman that needeth not be ashamed
rightly dividing the word of truth.
²Tim 2:15

Date:

Speaker:

Sermon Title:

Scripture Notes

Personal Revelation:

Appointments:

Tithe/Offering:

JOB

Study to show thyself approved unto God,
A workman that needeth not be ashamed
rightly dividing the word of truth.
²Tim 2:15

Date:

Speaker:

Sermon Title:

Scripture Notes

JOB

Personal Revelation:

Appointments:

Tithe/Offering:

Study to show thyself approved unto God,
A workman that needeth not be ashamed
rightly dividing the word of truth.
²Tim 2:15

Date:
Speaker:
Sermon Title:

Scripture Notes

Personal Revelation:

Appointments:

Tithe/Offering:

JOB

Study to show thyself approved unto God,
A workman that needeth not be ashamed
rightly dividing the word of truth.
²Tim 2:15

Date:
Speaker:
Sermon Title:

Scripture Notes

Personal Revelation:

Appointments:

Tithe/Offering:

JOB

Study to show thyself approved unto God,
A workman that needeth not be ashamed
rightly dividing the word of truth.
²Tim 2:15

Date:
Speaker:
Sermon Title:

Scripture Notes

Personal Revelation:

Appointments:

Tithe/Offering:

JOB

Study to show thyself approved unto God,
A workman that needeth not be ashamed
rightly dividing the word of truth.
²Tim 2:15

Date:

Speaker:

Sermon Title:

Scripture Notes

Personal Revelation:

Appointments:

Tithe/Offering:

JOB

Study to show thyself approved unto God,
A workman that needeth not be ashamed
rightly dividing the word of truth.
²Tim 2:15

Date:

Speaker:

Sermon Title:

Scripture Notes

Personal Revelation:

Appointments:

Tithe/Offering:

JOB

Study to show thyself approved unto God,
A workman that needeth not be ashamed
rightly dividing the word of truth.
²Tim 2:15

Date:
Speaker:
Sermon Title:

Scripture Notes

Personal Revelation:

Appointments:

Tithe/Offering:

PSALMS

> ***Study to show thyself approved unto God,***
> ***A workman that needeth not be ashamed***
> ***rightly dividing the word of truth.***
> *²Tim 2:15*

Date:
Speaker:
Sermon Title:

Scripture Notes

Personal Revelation:

Appointments:

Tithe/Offering:

PSALMS

Study to show thyself approved unto God,
A workman that needeth not be ashamed
rightly dividing the word of truth.
²Tim 2:15

Date:
Speaker:
Sermon Title:

Scripture Notes

Personal Revelation:

Appointments:

Tithe/Offering:

PSALMS

Study to show thyself approved unto God,
A workman that needeth not be ashamed
rightly dividing the word of truth.
²Tim 2:15

Date:
Speaker:
Sermon Title:

Scripture Notes

Personal Revelation:

Appointments:

Tithe/Offering:

PSALMS

Study to show thyself approved unto God,
A workman that needeth not be ashamed
rightly dividing the word of truth.
²Tim 2:15

Date:
Speaker:
Sermon Title:

Scripture Notes

PSALMS

Personal Revelation:

Appointments:

Tithe/Offering:

Study to show thyself approved unto God,
A workman that needeth not be ashamed
rightly dividing the word of truth.
²Tim 2:15

Date:

Speaker:

Sermon Title:

Scripture Notes

PSALMS

Personal Revelation:

Appointments:

Tithe/Offering:

Study to show thyself approved unto God, A workman that needeth not be ashamed rightly dividing the word of truth. *²Tim 2:15*	
Date: **Speaker:** **Sermon Title:**	
Scripture Notes	

Date:
Speaker:
Sermon Title:

Scripture Notes

PSALMS

Personal Revelation:

Appointments:

Tithe/Offering:

Study to show thyself approved unto God,
A workman that needeth not be ashamed
rightly dividing the word of truth.
²Tim 2:15

Date:
Speaker:
Sermon Title:

Scripture Notes

Personal Revelation:

Appointments:

Tithe/Offering:

PROVERBS

Study to show thyself approved unto God,
A workman that needeth not be ashamed
rightly dividing the word of truth.
²Tim 2:15

Date:
Speaker:
Sermon Title:

Scripture Notes

Personal Revelation:

Appointments:

Tithe/Offering:

PROVERBS

Study to show thyself approved unto God,
A workman that needeth not be ashamed
rightly dividing the word of truth.
²Tim 2:15

Date:
Speaker:
Sermon Title:

Scripture Notes

PROVERBS

Personal Revelation:

Appointments:

Tithe/Offering:

Study to show thyself approved unto God,
A workman that needeth not be ashamed
rightly dividing the word of truth.
²Tim 2:15

Date:
Speaker:
Sermon Title:

Scripture Notes

PROVERBS

Personal Revelation:

Appointments:

Tithe/Offering:

Darcell Lemmons

Study to show thyself approved unto God, A workman that needeth not be ashamed rightly dividing the word of truth. *²Tim 2:15*	
Date: **Speaker:** **Sermon Title:**	
Scripture Notes	
Personal Revelation:	
Appointments:	
Tithe/Offering:	

PROVERBS

Study to show thyself approved unto God,
A workman that needeth not be ashamed
rightly dividing the word of truth.
²Tim 2:15

Date:
Speaker:
Sermon Title:

Scripture Notes

Personal Revelation:

Appointments:

Tithe/Offering:

PROVERBS

Study to show thyself approved unto God,
A workman that needeth not be ashamed
rightly dividing the word of truth.
²Tim 2:15

Date:

Speaker:

Sermon Title:

Scripture Notes

Personal Revelation:

Appointments:

Tithe/Offering:

PROVERBS

Study to show thyself approved unto God,
A workman that needeth not be ashamed
rightly dividing the word of truth.
²Tim 2:15

Date:
Speaker:
Sermon Title:

Scripture Notes

Personal Revelation:

Appointments:

Tithe/Offering:

ECCLESIASTES

> *Study to show thyself approved unto God,*
> *A workman that needeth not be ashamed*
> *rightly dividing the word of truth.*
> *²Tim 2:15*

Date:

Speaker:

Sermon Title:

Scripture Notes

Personal Revelation:

Appointments:

Tithe/Offering:

ECCLESIASTES

Study to show thyself approved unto God,
A workman that needeth not be ashamed
rightly dividing the word of truth.
²Tim 2:15

Date:
Speaker:
Sermon Title:

Scripture Notes

Personal Revelation:

Appointments:

Tithe/Offering:

ECCLESIASTES

Study to show thyself approved unto God,
A workman that needeth not be ashamed
rightly dividing the word of truth.
²Tim 2:15

Date:
Speaker:
Sermon Title:

Scripture Notes

ECCLESIASTES

Personal Revelation:

Appointments:

Tithe/Offering:

Study to show thyself approved unto God,
A workman that needeth not be ashamed
rightly dividing the word of truth.
²Tim 2:15

Date:
Speaker:
Sermon Title:

Scripture Notes

Personal Revelation:

Appointments:

Tithe/Offering:

ECCLESIASTES

Study to show thyself approved unto God,
A workman that needeth not be ashamed
rightly dividing the word of truth.
²Tim 2:15

Date:

Speaker:

Sermon Title:

Scripture Notes

Personal Revelation:

Appointments:

Tithe/Offering:

ECCLESIASTES

Study to show thyself approved unto God,
A workman that needeth not be ashamed
rightly dividing the word of truth.
²Tim 2:15

Date:
Speaker:
Sermon Title:

Scripture Notes

Personal Revelation:

Appointments:

Tithe/Offering:

ECCLESIASTES

Study to show thyself approved unto God,
A workman that needeth not be ashamed
rightly dividing the word of truth.
²Tim 2:15

Date:
Speaker:
Sermon Title:

Scripture Notes

THE SONG OF SOLOMON

Personal Revelation:

Appointments:

Tithe/Offering:

Study to show thyself approved unto God,
A workman that needeth not be ashamed
rightly dividing the word of truth.
²Tim 2:15

Date:

Speaker:

Sermon Title:

Scripture Notes

Personal Revelation:

Appointments:

Tithe/Offering:

THE SONG OF SOLOMON

Darcell Lemmons

Study to show thyself approved unto God,
A workman that needeth not be ashamed
rightly dividing the word of truth.
²Tim 2:15

Date:
Speaker:
Sermon Title:

Scripture Notes

Personal Revelation:

Appointments:

Tithe/Offering:

THE SONG OF SOLOMON

Study to show thyself approved unto God,
A workman that needeth not be ashamed
rightly dividing the word of truth.
²Tim 2:15

Date:
Speaker:
Sermon Title:

Scripture Notes

Personal Revelation:

Appointments:

Tithe/Offering:

THE SONG OF SOLOMON

Darcell Lemmons

Study to show thyself approved unto God,
A workman that needeth not be ashamed
rightly dividing the word of truth.
²Tim 2:15

Date:
Speaker:
Sermon Title:

Scripture Notes

Personal Revelation:

Appointments:

Tithe/Offering:

THE SONG OF SOLOMON

Study to show thyself approved unto God,
A workman that needeth not be ashamed
rightly dividing the word of truth.
²Tim 2:15

Date:
Speaker:
Sermon Title:

Scripture Notes

Personal Revelation:

Appointments:

Tithe/Offering:

THE SONG OF SOLOMON

> *Study to show thyself approved unto God,*
> *A workman that needeth not be ashamed*
> *rightly dividing the word of truth.*
> *²Tim 2:15*

Date:
Speaker:
Sermon Title:

Scripture Notes

Personal Revelation:

Appointments:

Tithe/Offering:

THE SONG OF SOLOMON

Study to show thyself approved unto God,
A workman that needeth not be ashamed
rightly dividing the word of truth.
²Tim 2:15

Date:
Speaker:
Sermon Title:

Scripture Notes

ISAIAH

Personal Revelation:

Appointments:

Tithe/Offering:

Study to show thyself approved unto God,
A workman that needeth not be ashamed
rightly dividing the word of truth.
²Tim 2:15

Date:
Speaker:
Sermon Title:

Scripture Notes

Personal Revelation:

Appointments:

Tithe/Offering:

ISAIAH

Study to show thyself approved unto God,
A workman that needeth not be ashamed
rightly dividing the word of truth.
²Tim 2:15

Date:
Speaker:
Sermon Title:

Scripture Notes

Personal Revelation:

Appointments:

Tithe/Offering:

ISAIAH

Study to show thyself approved unto God,
A workman that needeth not be ashamed
rightly dividing the word of truth.
²Tim 2:15

Date:

Speaker:

Sermon Title:

Scripture Notes

Personal Revelation:

Appointments:

Tithe/Offering:

ISAIAH

Study to show thyself approved unto God,
A workman that needeth not be ashamed
rightly dividing the word of truth.
²Tim 2:15

Date:
Speaker:
Sermon Title:

Scripture Notes

Personal Revelation:

Appointments:

Tithe/Offering:

ISAIAH

> *Study to show thyself approved unto God,*
> *A workman that needeth not be ashamed*
> *rightly dividing the word of truth.*
> *²Tim 2:15*

Date:

Speaker:

Sermon Title:

Scripture Notes

Personal Revelation:

Appointments:

Tithe/Offering:

ISAIAH

Study to show thyself approved unto God,
A workman that needeth not be ashamed
rightly dividing the word of truth.
²Tim 2:15

Date:
Speaker:
Sermon Title:

Scripture Notes

Personal Revelation:

Appointments:

Tithe/Offering:

ISAIAH

Darcell Lemmons

Study to show thyself approved unto God,
A workman that needeth not be ashamed
rightly dividing the word of truth.
²Tim 2:15

Date:
Speaker:
Sermon Title:

Scripture Notes

JEREMIAH

Personal Revelation:

Appointments:

Tithe/Offering:

> *Study to show thyself approved unto God,*
> *A workman that needeth not be ashamed*
> *rightly dividing the word of truth.*
> *²Tim 2:15*

Date:
Speaker:
Sermon Title:

Scripture Notes

Personal Revelation:

Appointments:

Tithe/Offering:

JEREMIAH

Study to show thyself approved unto God,
A workman that needeth not be ashamed
rightly dividing the word of truth.
²Tim 2:15

Date:

Speaker:

Sermon Title:

Scripture Notes

JEREMIAH

Personal Revelation:

Appointments:

Tithe/Offering:

Study to show thyself approved unto God,
A workman that needeth not be ashamed
rightly dividing the word of truth.
²Tim 2:15

Date:

Speaker:

Sermon Title:

Scripture Notes

Personal Revelation:

Appointments:

Tithe/Offering:

JEREMIAH

> *Study to show thyself approved unto God,*
> *A workman that needeth not be ashamed*
> *rightly dividing the word of truth.*
> *²Tim 2:15*

Date:
Speaker:
Sermon Title:

Scripture Notes

JEREMIAH

Personal Revelation:

Appointments:

Tithe/Offering:

Study to show thyself approved unto God,
A workman that needeth not be ashamed
rightly dividing the word of truth.
²Tim 2:15

Date:
Speaker:
Sermon Title:

Scripture Notes

Personal Revelation:

Appointments:

Tithe/Offering:

JEREMIAH

> *Study to show thyself approved unto God,*
> *A workman that needeth not be ashamed*
> *rightly dividing the word of truth.*
> *²Tim 2:15*

Date:
Speaker:
Sermon Title:

Scripture Notes

JEREMIAH

Personal Revelation:

Appointments:

Tithe/Offering:

Study to show thyself approved unto God,
A workman that needeth not be ashamed
rightly dividing the word of truth.
²Tim 2:15

Date:
Speaker:
Sermon Title:

Scripture Notes

Personal Revelation:

Appointments:

Tithe/Offering:

THE LAMENTATIONS

> *Study to show thyself approved unto God,*
> *A workman that needeth not be ashamed*
> *rightly dividing the word of truth.*
> *²Tim 2:15*

Date:
Speaker:
Sermon Title:

Scripture Notes

THE LAMENTATIONS

Personal Revelation:

Appointments:

Tithe/Offering:

Study to show thyself approved unto God,
A workman that needeth not be ashamed
rightly dividing the word of truth.
²Tim 2:15

Date:
Speaker:
Sermon Title:

Scripture Notes

Personal Revelation:

Appointments:

Tithe/Offering:

THE LAMENTATIONS

> *Study to show thyself approved unto God,*
> *A workman that needeth not be ashamed*
> *rightly dividing the word of truth.*
> *²Tim 2:15*

Date:
Speaker:
Sermon Title:

Scripture Notes

THE LAMENTATIONS

Personal Revelation:

Appointments:

Tithe/Offering:

Study to show thyself approved unto God,
A workman that needeth not be ashamed
rightly dividing the word of truth.
²Tim 2:15

Date:

Speaker:

Sermon Title:

Scripture Notes

Personal Revelation:

Appointments:

Tithe/Offering:

THE LAMENTATIONS

Study to show thyself approved unto God,
A workman that needeth not be ashamed
rightly dividing the word of truth.
²Tim 2:15

Date:
Speaker:
Sermon Title:

Scripture Notes

THE LAMENTATIONS

Personal Revelation:

Appointments:

Tithe/Offering:

Study to show thyself approved unto God,
A workman that needeth not be ashamed
rightly dividing the word of truth.
²Tim 2:15

Date:
Speaker:
Sermon Title:

Scripture Notes

Personal Revelation:

Appointments:

Tithe/Offering:

THE LAMENTATIONS

Study to show thyself approved unto God,
A workman that needeth not be ashamed
rightly dividing the word of truth.
²Tim 2:15

Date:
Speaker:
Sermon Title:

Scripture Notes

EZEKIEL

Personal Revelation:

Appointments:

Tithe/Offering:

Study to show thyself approved unto God,
A workman that needeth not be ashamed
rightly dividing the word of truth.
2Tim 2:15

Date:
Speaker:
Sermon Title:

Scripture Notes

Personal Revelation:

Appointments:

Tithe/Offering:

EZEKIEL

> ***Study to show thyself approved unto God,***
> ***A workman that needeth not be ashamed***
> ***rightly dividing the word of truth.***
> *²Tim 2:15*

Date:

Speaker:

Sermon Title:

Scripture Notes

EZEKIEL

Personal Revelation:

Appointments:

Tithe/Offering:

Study to show thyself approved unto God,
A workman that needeth not be ashamed
rightly dividing the word of truth.
²Tim 2:15

Date:
Speaker:
Sermon Title:

Scripture Notes

Personal Revelation:

Appointments:

Tithe/Offering:

EZEKIEL

Study to show thyself approved unto God,
A workman that needeth not be ashamed
rightly dividing the word of truth.
²Tim 2:15

Date:
Speaker:
Sermon Title:

Scripture Notes

EZEKIEL

Personal Revelation:

Appointments:

Tithe/Offering:

Study to show thyself approved unto God,
A workman that needeth not be ashamed
rightly dividing the word of truth.
²Tim 2:15

Date:
Speaker:
Sermon Title:

Scripture Notes

Personal Revelation:

Appointments:

Tithe/Offering:

EZEKIEL

Study to show thyself approved unto God,
A workman that needeth not be ashamed
rightly dividing the word of truth.
²Tim 2:15

Date:
Speaker:
Sermon Title:

Scripture Notes

Personal Revelation:

Appointments:

Tithe/Offering:

EZEKIEL

Study to show thyself approved unto God,
A workman that needeth not be ashamed
rightly dividing the word of truth.
²Tim 2:15

Date:
Speaker:
Sermon Title:

Scripture Notes

DANIEL

Personal Revelation:

Appointments:

Tithe/Offering:

Study to show thyself approved unto God, A workman that needeth not be ashamed rightly dividing the word of truth. *²Tim 2:15*

Date:
Speaker:
Sermon Title:

Scripture Notes

DANIEL

Personal Revelation:

Appointments:

Tithe/Offering:

Study to show thyself approved unto God,
A workman that needeth not be ashamed
rightly dividing the word of truth.
²Tim 2:15

Date:
Speaker:
Sermon Title:

Scripture Notes

DANIEL

Personal Revelation:

Appointments:

Tithe/Offering:

Study to show thyself approved unto God,
A workman that needeth not be ashamed
rightly dividing the word of truth.
²Tim 2:15

Date:
Speaker:
Sermon Title:

Scripture Notes

DANIEL

Personal Revelation:

Appointments:

Tithe/Offering:

Study to show thyself approved unto God,
A workman that needeth not be ashamed
rightly dividing the word of truth.
²Tim 2:15

Date:
Speaker:
Sermon Title:

Scripture Notes

Personal Revelation:

Appointments:

Tithe/Offering:

DANIEL

Study to show thyself approved unto God,
A workman that needeth not be ashamed
rightly dividing the word of truth.
²Tim 2:15

Date:
Speaker:
Sermon Title:

Scripture Notes

Personal Revelation:

Appointments:

Tithe/Offering:

DANIEL

Study to show thyself approved unto God,
A workman that needeth not be ashamed
rightly dividing the word of truth.
²Tim 2:15

Date:
Speaker:
Sermon Title:

Scripture Notes

Personal Revelation:

Appointments:

Tithe/Offering:

DANIEL

Study to show thyself approved unto God,
A workman that needeth not be ashamed
rightly dividing the word of truth.
²Tim 2:15

Date:
Speaker:
Sermon Title:

Scripture Notes

Personal Revelation:

Appointments:

Tithe/Offering:

HOSEA

Study to show thyself approved unto God,
A workman that needeth not be ashamed
rightly dividing the word of truth.
²Tim 2:15

Date:

Speaker:

Sermon Title:

Scripture Notes

Personal Revelation:

Appointments:

Tithe/Offering:

HOSEA

Study to show thyself approved unto God,
A workman that needeth not be ashamed
rightly dividing the word of truth.
²Tim 2:15

Date:
Speaker:
Sermon Title:

Scripture Notes

Personal Revelation:

Appointments:

Tithe/Offering:

HOSEA

Study to show thyself approved unto God,
A workman that needeth not be ashamed
rightly dividing the word of truth.
²Tim 2:15

Date:

Speaker:

Sermon Title:

Scripture Notes

Personal Revelation:

Appointments:

Tithe/Offering:

HOSEA

Study to show thyself approved unto God,
A workman that needeth not be ashamed
rightly dividing the word of truth.
²Tim 2:15

Date:
Speaker:
Sermon Title:

Scripture Notes

HOSEA

Personal Revelation:

Appointments:

Tithe/Offering:

Study to show thyself approved unto God,
A workman that needeth not be ashamed
rightly dividing the word of truth.
²Tim 2:15

Date:
Speaker:
Sermon Title:

Scripture Notes

Personal Revelation:

Appointments:

Tithe/Offering:

HOSEA

Study to show thyself approved unto God,
A workman that needeth not be ashamed
rightly dividing the word of truth.
²Tim 2:15

Date:
Speaker:
Sermon Title:

Scripture Notes

HOSEA

Personal Revelation:

Appointments:

Tithe/Offering:

Study to show thyself approved unto God,
A workman that needeth not be ashamed
rightly dividing the word of truth.
²Tim 2:15

Date:
Speaker:
Sermon Title:

Scripture Notes

Personal Revelation:

Appointments:

Tithe/Offering:

JOEL

Darcell Lemmons

Study to show thyself approved unto God,
A workman that needeth not be ashamed
rightly dividing the word of truth.
²Tim 2:15

Date:
Speaker:
Sermon Title:

Scripture Notes

JOEL

Personal Revelation:

Appointments:

Tithe/Offering:

Study to show thyself approved unto God,
A workman that needeth not be ashamed
rightly dividing the word of truth.
²Tim 2:15

Date:
Speaker:
Sermon Title:

Scripture Notes

Personal Revelation:

Appointments:

Tithe/Offering:

JOEL

Study to show thyself approved unto God,
A workman that needeth not be ashamed
rightly dividing the word of truth.
²Tim 2:15

Date:
Speaker:
Sermon Title:

Scripture Notes

JOEL

Personal Revelation:

Appointments:

Tithe/Offering:

Study to show thyself approved unto God,
A workman that needeth not be ashamed
rightly dividing the word of truth.
²Tim 2:15

Date:
Speaker:
Sermon Title:

Scripture Notes

JOEL

Personal Revelation:

Appointments:

Tithe/Offering:

Darcell Lemmons

Study to show thyself approved unto God, A workman that needeth not be ashamed rightly dividing the word of truth. *²Tim 2:15*	
Date: **Speaker:** **Sermon Title:**	
Scripture Notes	
	JOEL
Personal Revelation:	
Appointments:	
Tithe/Offering:	

Study to show thyself approved unto God,
A workman that needeth not be ashamed
rightly dividing the word of truth.
²Tim 2:15

Date:
Speaker:
Sermon Title:

Scripture Notes

Personal Revelation:

Appointments:

Tithe/Offering:

JOEL

Study to show thyself approved unto God,
A workman that needeth not be ashamed
rightly dividing the word of truth.
²Tim 2:15

Date:
Speaker:
Sermon Title:

Scripture Notes

AMOS

Personal Revelation:

Appointments:

Tithe/Offering:

Study to show thyself approved unto God,
A workman that needeth not be ashamed
rightly dividing the word of truth.
²Tim 2:15

Date:
Speaker:
Sermon Title:

Scripture Notes

AMOS

Personal Revelation:

Appointments:

Tithe/Offering:

Study to show thyself approved unto God,
A workman that needeth not be ashamed
rightly dividing the word of truth.
²Tim 2:15

Date:

Speaker:

Sermon Title:

Scripture Notes

AMOS

Personal Revelation:

Appointments:

Tithe/Offering:

Study to show thyself approved unto God,
A workman that needeth not be ashamed
rightly dividing the word of truth.
²Tim 2:15

Date:
Speaker:
Sermon Title:

Scripture Notes

Personal Revelation:

Appointments:

Tithe/Offering:

AMOS

Study to show thyself approved unto God,
A workman that needeth not be ashamed
rightly dividing the word of truth.
²Tim 2:15

Date:
Speaker:
Sermon Title:

Scripture Notes

AMOS

Personal Revelation:

Appointments:

Tithe/Offering:

Study to show thyself approved unto God,
A workman that needeth not be ashamed
rightly dividing the word of truth.
²Tim 2:15

Date:
Speaker:
Sermon Title:

Scripture Notes

Personal Revelation:

Appointments:

Tithe/Offering:

AMOS

Darcell Lemmons

Study to show thyself approved unto God, A workman that needeth not be ashamed rightly dividing the word of truth.   *²Tim 2:15*

Date:
Speaker:
Sermon Title:

Scripture Notes

AMOS

Personal Revelation:

Appointments:

Tithe/Offering:

218

Study to show thyself approved unto God,
A workman that needeth not be ashamed
rightly dividing the word of truth.
²Tim 2:15

Date:
Speaker:
Sermon Title:

Scripture Notes

OBADIAH

Personal Revelation:

Appointments:

Tithe/Offering:

Study to show thyself approved unto God, A workman that needeth not be ashamed rightly dividing the word of truth. *²Tim 2:15*	
Date: **Speaker:** **Sermon Title:**	
Scripture Notes	**OBADIAH**
Personal Revelation:	
Appointments:	
Tithe/Offering:	

Study to show thyself approved unto God,
A workman that needeth not be ashamed
rightly dividing the word of truth.
²Tim 2:15

Date:
Speaker:
Sermon Title:

Scripture Notes

Personal Revelation:

Appointments:

Tithe/Offering:

OBADIAH

Study to show thyself approved unto God,
A workman that needeth not be ashamed
rightly dividing the word of truth.
²Tim 2:15

Date:
Speaker:
Sermon Title:

Scripture Notes

OBADIAH

Personal Revelation:

Appointments:

Tithe/Offering:

Study to show thyself approved unto God,
A workman that needeth not be ashamed
rightly dividing the word of truth.
²Tim 2:15

Date:
Speaker:
Sermon Title:

Scripture Notes

Personal Revelation:

Appointments:

Tithe/Offering:

OBADIAH

Darcell Lemmons

Study to show thyself approved unto God,
A workman that needeth not be ashamed
rightly dividing the word of truth.
²Tim 2:15

Date:
Speaker:
Sermon Title:

Scripture Notes

OBADIAH

Personal Revelation:

Appointments:

Tithe/Offering:

Study to show thyself approved unto God,
A workman that needeth not be ashamed
rightly dividing the word of truth.
²Tim 2:15

Date:
Speaker:
Sermon Title:

Scripture Notes

OBADIAH

Personal Revelation:

Appointments:

Tithe/Offering:

Darcell Lemmons

> *Study to show thyself approved unto God,*
> *A workman that needeth not be ashamed*
> *rightly dividing the word of truth.*
> *²Tim 2:15*

Date:
Speaker:
Sermon Title:

Scripture Notes

JONAH

Personal Revelation:

Appointments:

Tithe/Offering:

Study to show thyself approved unto God,
A workman that needeth not be ashamed
rightly dividing the word of truth.
²Tim 2:15

Date:
Speaker:
Sermon Title:

Scripture Notes

JONAH

Personal Revelation:

Appointments:

Tithe/Offering:

> *Study to show thyself approved unto God,*
> *A workman that needeth not be ashamed*
> *rightly dividing the word of truth.*
> *²Tim 2:15*

Date:
Speaker:
Sermon Title:

Scripture Notes

Personal Revelation:

Appointments:

Tithe/Offering:

JONAH

Study to show thyself approved unto God,
A workman that needeth not be ashamed
rightly dividing the word of truth.
²Tim 2:15

Date:
Speaker:
Sermon Title:

Scripture Notes

Personal Revelation:

Appointments:

Tithe/Offering:

JONAH

Darcell Lemmons

Study to show thyself approved unto God,
A workman that needeth not be ashamed
rightly dividing the word of truth.
²Tim 2:15

Date:
Speaker:
Sermon Title:

Scripture Notes

JONAH

Personal Revelation:

Appointments:

Tithe/Offering:

Study to show thyself approved unto God,
A workman that needeth not be ashamed
rightly dividing the word of truth.
²Tim 2:15

Date:
Speaker:
Sermon Title:

Scripture Notes

Personal Revelation:

Appointments:

Tithe/Offering:

JONAH

Study to show thyself approved unto God,
A workman that needeth not be ashamed
rightly dividing the word of truth.
²Tim 2:15

Date:
Speaker:
Sermon Title:

Scripture Notes

JONAH

Personal Revelation:

Appointments:

Tithe/Offering:

Study to show thyself approved unto God,
A workman that needeth not be ashamed
rightly dividing the word of truth.
²Tim 2:15

Date:

Speaker:

Sermon Title:

Scripture Notes

Personal Revelation:

Appointments:

Tithe/Offering:

MICAH

Study to show thyself approved unto God,
A workman that needeth not be ashamed
rightly dividing the word of truth.
²Tim 2:15

Date:
Speaker:
Sermon Title:

Scripture Notes

MICAH

Personal Revelation:

Appointments:

Tithe/Offering:

Study to show thyself approved unto God,
A workman that needeth not be ashamed
rightly dividing the word of truth.
2Tim 2:15

Date:
Speaker:
Sermon Title:

Scripture Notes

Personal Revelation:

Appointments:

Tithe/Offering:

MICAH

Study to show thyself approved unto God,
A workman that needeth not be ashamed
rightly dividing the word of truth.
²Tim 2:15

Date:

Speaker:

Sermon Title:

Scripture Notes

MICAH

Personal Revelation:

Appointments:

Tithe/Offering:

Study to show thyself approved unto God,
A workman that needeth not be ashamed
rightly dividing the word of truth.
²Tim 2:15

Date:
Speaker:
Sermon Title:

Scripture Notes

Personal Revelation:

Appointments:

Tithe/Offering:

MICAH

Study to show thyself approved unto God,
A workman that needeth not be ashamed
rightly dividing the word of truth.
²Tim 2:15

Date:

Speaker:

Sermon Title:

Scripture Notes

MICAH

Personal Revelation:

Appointments:

Tithe/Offering:

Study to show thyself approved unto God,
A workman that needeth not be ashamed
rightly dividing the word of truth.
²Tim 2:15

Date:
Speaker:
Sermon Title:

Scripture Notes

Personal Revelation:

Appointments:

Tithe/Offering:

MICAH

Study to show thyself approved unto God,
A workman that needeth not be ashamed
rightly dividing the word of truth.
²Tim 2:15

Date:
Speaker:
Sermon Title:

Scripture Notes

NAHUM

Personal Revelation:

Appointments:

Tithe/Offering:

Study to show thyself approved unto God,
A workman that needeth not be ashamed
rightly dividing the word of truth.
²Tim 2:15

Date:
Speaker:
Sermon Title:

Scripture Notes

Personal Revelation:

Appointments:

Tithe/Offering:

NAHUM

Study to show thyself approved unto God,
A workman that needeth not be ashamed
rightly dividing the word of truth.
²Tim 2:15

Date:
Speaker:
Sermon Title:

Scripture Notes

NAHUM

Personal Revelation:

Appointments:

Tithe/Offering:

Study to show thyself approved unto God,
A workman that needeth not be ashamed
rightly dividing the word of truth.
²Tim 2:15

Date:
Speaker:
Sermon Title:

Scripture Notes

Personal Revelation:

Appointments:

Tithe/Offering:

NAHUM

Study to show thyself approved unto God,
A workman that needeth not be ashamed
rightly dividing the word of truth.
²Tim 2:15

Date:
Speaker:
Sermon Title:

Scripture Notes

Personal Revelation:

Appointments:

Tithe/Offering:

NAHUM

Study to show thyself approved unto God,
A workman that needeth not be ashamed
rightly dividing the word of truth.
²Tim 2:15

Date:
Speaker:
Sermon Title:

Scripture Notes

Personal Revelation:

Appointments:

Tithe/Offering:

NAHUM

Study to show thyself approved unto God,
A workman that needeth not be ashamed
rightly dividing the word of truth.
²Tim 2:15

Date:
Speaker:
Sermon Title:

Scripture Notes

Personal Revelation:

Appointments:

Tithe/Offering:

NAHUM

> *Study to show thyself approved unto God,*
> *A workman that needeth not be ashamed*
> *rightly dividing the word of truth.*
> *²Tim 2:15*

Date:

Speaker:

Sermon Title:

Scripture Notes

HABAKKUK

Personal Revelation:

Appointments:

Tithe/Offering:

Study to show thyself approved unto God,
A workman that needeth not be ashamed
rightly dividing the word of truth.
²Tim 2:15

Date:
Speaker:
Sermon Title:

Scripture Notes

Personal Revelation:

Appointments:

Tithe/Offering:

HABAKKUK

Study to show thyself approved unto God,
A workman that needeth not be ashamed
rightly dividing the word of truth.
²Tim 2:15

Date:
Speaker:
Sermon Title:

Scripture Notes

Personal Revelation:

Appointments:

Tithe/Offering:

HABAKKUK

Study to show thyself approved unto God,
A workman that needeth not be ashamed
rightly dividing the word of truth.
²Tim 2:15

Date:
Speaker:
Sermon Title:

Scripture Notes

HABAKKUK

Personal Revelation:

Appointments:

Tithe/Offering:

Study to show thyself approved unto God,
A workman that needeth not be ashamed
rightly dividing the word of truth.
²Tim 2:15

Date:
Speaker:
Sermon Title:

Scripture Notes

HABAKKUK

Personal Revelation:

Appointments:

Tithe/Offering:

Study to show thyself approved unto God,
A workman that needeth not be ashamed
rightly dividing the word of truth.
²Tim 2:15

Date:
Speaker:
Sermon Title:

Scripture Notes

Personal Revelation:

Appointments:

Tithe/Offering:

HABAKKUK

Study to show thyself approved unto God,
A workman that needeth not be ashamed
rightly dividing the word of truth.
²Tim 2:15

Date:
Speaker:
Sermon Title:

Scripture Notes

HABAKKUK

Personal Revelation:

Appointments:

Tithe/Offering:

Study to show thyself approved unto God,
A workman that needeth not be ashamed
rightly dividing the word of truth.
²Tim 2:15

Date:
Speaker:
Sermon Title:

Scripture Notes

ZEPHANIAH

Personal Revelation:

Appointments:

Tithe/Offering:

Study to show thyself approved unto God,
A workman that needeth not be ashamed
rightly dividing the word of truth.
²Tim 2:15

Date:
Speaker:
Sermon Title:

Scripture Notes

ZEPHANIAH

Personal Revelation:

Appointments:

Tithe/Offering:

Darcell Lemmons

Study to show thyself approved unto God,
A workman that needeth not be ashamed
rightly dividing the word of truth.
²Tim 2:15

Date:
Speaker:
Sermon Title:

Scripture Notes

ZEPHANIAH

Personal Revelation:

Appointments:

Tithe/Offering:

> *Study to show thyself approved unto God,*
> *A workman that needeth not be ashamed*
> *rightly dividing the word of truth.*
> *²Tim 2:15*

Date:
Speaker:
Sermon Title:

Scripture Notes

ZEPHANIAH

Personal Revelation:

Appointments:

Tithe/Offering:

> *Study to show thyself approved unto God,*
> *A workman that needeth not be ashamed*
> *rightly dividing the word of truth.*
> *²Tim 2:15*

Date:

Speaker:

Sermon Title:

Scripture Notes

Personal Revelation:

Appointments:

Tithe/Offering:

ZEPHANIAH

Study to show thyself approved unto God,
A workman that needeth not be ashamed
rightly dividing the word of truth.
2Tim 2:15

Date:
Speaker:
Sermon Title:

Scripture Notes

ZEPHANIAH

Personal Revelation:

Appointments:

Tithe/Offering:

Study to show thyself approved unto God,
A workman that needeth not be ashamed
rightly dividing the word of truth.
²Tim 2:15

Date:
Speaker:
Sermon Title:

Scripture Notes

Personal Revelation:

Appointments:

Tithe/Offering:

ZEPHANIAH

Study to show thyself approved unto God,
A workman that needeth not be ashamed
rightly dividing the word of truth.
²Tim 2:15

Date:
Speaker:
Sermon Title:

Scripture Notes

Personal Revelation:

Appointments:

Tithe/Offering:

HAGGAI

Study to show thyself approved unto God,
A workman that needeth not be ashamed
rightly dividing the word of truth.
²Tim 2:15

Date:
Speaker:
Sermon Title:

Scripture Notes

HAGGAI

Personal Revelation:

Appointments:

Tithe/Offering:

Study to show thyself approved unto God,
A workman that needeth not be ashamed
rightly dividing the word of truth.
²Tim 2:15

Date:

Speaker:

Sermon Title:

Scripture Notes

Personal Revelation:

Appointments:

Tithe/Offering:

HAGGAI

Darcell Lemmons

> *Study to show thyself approved unto God,*
> *A workman that needeth not be ashamed*
> *rightly dividing the word of truth.*
> *²Tim 2:15*

Date:
Speaker:
Sermon Title:

Scripture Notes

HAGGAI

Personal Revelation:

Appointments:

Tithe/Offering:

Study to show thyself approved unto God,
A workman that needeth not be ashamed
rightly dividing the word of truth.
²Tim 2:15

Date:

Speaker:

Sermon Title:

Scripture Notes

HAGGAI

Personal Revelation:

Appointments:

Tithe/Offering:

Study to show thyself approved unto God,
A workman that needeth not be ashamed
rightly dividing the word of truth.
²Tim 2:15

Date:
Speaker:
Sermon Title:

Scripture Notes

Personal Revelation:

Appointments:

Tithe/Offering:

HAGGAI

Study to show thyself approved unto God,
A workman that needeth not be ashamed
rightly dividing the word of truth.
²Tim 2:15

Date:
Speaker:
Sermon Title:

Scripture Notes

HAGGAI

Personal Revelation:

Appointments:

Tithe/Offering:

Study to show thyself approved unto God,
A workman that needeth not be ashamed
rightly dividing the word of truth.
²Tim 2:15

Date:
Speaker:
Sermon Title:

Scripture Notes

ZECHARIAH

Personal Revelation:

Appointments:

Tithe/Offering:

Study to show thyself approved unto God,
A workman that needeth not be ashamed
rightly dividing the word of truth.
²Tim 2:15

Date:
Speaker:
Sermon Title:

Scripture Notes

ZECHARIAH

Personal Revelation:

Appointments:

Tithe/Offering:

*Study to show thyself approved unto God,
A workman that needeth not be ashamed
rightly dividing the word of truth.*
²Tim 2:15

Date:
Speaker:
Sermon Title:

Scripture Notes

Personal Revelation:

Appointments:

Tithe/Offering:

ZECHARIAH

Study to show thyself approved unto God,
A workman that needeth not be ashamed
rightly dividing the word of truth.
²Tim 2:15

Date:

Speaker:

Sermon Title:

Scripture Notes

ZECHARIAH

Personal Revelation:

Appointments:

Tithe/Offering:

Darcell Lemmons

Study to show thyself approved unto God, A workman that needeth not be ashamed rightly dividing the word of truth. *²Tim 2:15*	
Date: **Speaker:** **Sermon Title:**	
Scripture Notes	

Date:
Speaker:
Sermon Title:

Scripture Notes

Personal Revelation:

Appointments:

Tithe/Offering:

ZECHARIAH

Study to show thyself approved unto God,
A workman that needeth not be ashamed
rightly dividing the word of truth.
²Tim 2:15

Date:
Speaker:
Sermon Title:

Scripture Notes

Personal Revelation:

Appointments:

Tithe/Offering:

ZECHARIAH

Study to show thyself approved unto God,
A workman that needeth not be ashamed
rightly dividing the word of truth.
²Tim 2:15

Date:
Speaker:
Sermon Title:

Scripture Notes

ZECHARIAH

Personal Revelation:

Appointments:

Tithe/Offering:

Study to show thyself approved unto God,
A workman that needeth not be ashamed
rightly dividing the word of truth.
²Tim 2:15

Date:

Speaker:

Sermon Title:

Scripture Notes

Personal Revelation:

Appointments:

Tithe/Offering:

MALACHI

Study to show thyself approved unto God,
A workman that needeth not be ashamed
rightly dividing the word of truth.
²Tim 2:15

Date:
Speaker:
Sermon Title:

Scripture Notes

MALACHI

Personal Revelation:

Appointments:

Tithe/Offering:

Study to show thyself approved unto God,
A workman that needeth not be ashamed
rightly dividing the word of truth.
²Tim 2:15

Date:
Speaker:
Sermon Title:

Scripture Notes

Personal Revelation:

Appointments:

Tithe/Offering:

MALACHI

Study to show thyself approved unto God,
A workman that needeth not be ashamed
rightly dividing the word of truth.
²Tim 2:15

Date:
Speaker:
Sermon Title:

Scripture Notes

Personal Revelation:

Appointments:

Tithe/Offering:

MALACHI

Study to show thyself approved unto God,
A workman that needeth not be ashamed
rightly dividing the word of truth.
²Tim 2:15

Date:

Speaker:

Sermon Title:

Scripture Notes

Personal Revelation:

Appointments:

Tithe/Offering:

MALACHI

Study to show thyself approved unto God,
A workman that needeth not be ashamed
rightly dividing the word of truth.
²Tim 2:15

Date:

Speaker:

Sermon Title:

Scripture Notes

Personal Revelation:

Appointments:

Tithe/Offering:

MALACHI

Study to show thyself approved unto God,
A workman that needeth not be ashamed
rightly dividing the word of truth.
²Tim 2:15

Date:
Speaker:
Sermon Title:

Scripture Notes

Personal Revelation:

Appointments:

Tithe/Offering:

MALACHI

The New Testament

Scripture Notes

Golden Nuggets

Telephone Contacts

Study to show thyself approved unto God,
A workman that needeth not be ashamed
rightly dividing the word of truth.
²Tim 2:15

Date:
Speaker:
Sermon Title:

Scripture Notes

Personal Revelation:

Appointments:

Tithe/Offering:

MATTHEW

> *Study to show thyself approved unto God,*
> *A workman that needeth not be ashamed*
> *rightly dividing the word of truth.*
> *²Tim 2:15*

Date:
Speaker:
Sermon Title:

Scripture Notes

MATTHEW

Personal Revelation:

Appointments:

Tithe/Offering:

Study to show thyself approved unto God,
A workman that needeth not be ashamed
rightly dividing the word of truth.
²Tim 2:15

Date:
Speaker:
Sermon Title:

Scripture Notes

Personal Revelation:

Appointments:

Tithe/Offering:

MATTHEW

Study to show thyself approved unto God,
A workman that needeth not be ashamed
rightly dividing the word of truth.
²Tim 2:15

Date:

Speaker:

Sermon Title:

Scripture Notes

MATTHEW

Personal Revelation:

Appointments:

Tithe/Offering:

Study to show thyself approved unto God,
A workman that needeth not be ashamed
rightly dividing the word of truth.
²Tim 2:15

Date:
Speaker:
Sermon Title:

Scripture Notes

Personal Revelation:

Appointments:

Tithe/Offering:

MATTHEW

Study to show thyself approved unto God,
A workman that needeth not be ashamed
rightly dividing the word of truth.
²Tim 2:15

Date:
Speaker:
Sermon Title:

Scripture Notes

MATTHEW

Personal Revelation:

Appointments:

Tithe/Offering:

Study to show thyself approved unto God,
A workman that needeth not be ashamed
rightly dividing the word of truth.
²Tim 2:15

Date:
Speaker:
Sermon Title:

Scripture Notes

Personal Revelation:

Appointments:

Tithe/Offering:

MATTHEW

Study to show thyself approved unto God,
A workman that needeth not be ashamed
rightly dividing the word of truth.
2Tim 2:15

Date:
Speaker:
Sermon Title:

Scripture Notes

Personal Revelation:

Appointments:

Tithe/Offering:

MARK

Study to show thyself approved unto God,
A workman that needeth not be ashamed
rightly dividing the word of truth.
²Tim 2:15

Date:

Speaker:

Sermon Title:

Scripture Notes

Personal Revelation:

Appointments:

Tithe/Offering:

MARK

Study to show thyself approved unto God,
A workman that needeth not be ashamed
rightly dividing the word of truth.
²Tim 2:15

Date:
Speaker:
Sermon Title:

Scripture Notes

Personal Revelation:

Appointments:

Tithe/Offering:

MARK

Study to show thyself approved unto God,
A workman that needeth not be ashamed
rightly dividing the word of truth.
²Tim 2:15

Date:
Speaker:
Sermon Title:

Scripture Notes

Personal Revelation:

Appointments:

Tithe/Offering:

MARK

Study to show thyself approved unto God,
A workman that needeth not be ashamed
rightly dividing the word of truth.
²Tim 2:15

Date:
Speaker:
Sermon Title:

Scripture Notes

Personal Revelation:

Appointments:

Tithe/Offering:

MARK

Study to show thyself approved unto God,
A workman that needeth not be ashamed
rightly dividing the word of truth.
²Tim 2:15

Date:

Speaker:

Sermon Title:

Scripture Notes

Personal Revelation:

Appointments:

Tithe/Offering:

MARK

Darcell Lemmons

> ***Study to show thyself approved unto God,***
> ***A workman that needeth not be ashamed***
> ***rightly dividing the word of truth.***
> *²Tim 2:15*

Date:
Speaker:
Sermon Title:

Scripture Notes

Personal Revelation:

Appointments:

Tithe/Offering:

MARK

Study to show thyself approved unto God,
A workman that needeth not be ashamed
rightly dividing the word of truth.
²Tim 2:15

Date:
Speaker:
Sermon Title:

Scripture Notes

LUKE

Personal Revelation:

Appointments:

Tithe/Offering:

Study to show thyself approved unto God,
A workman that needeth not be ashamed
rightly dividing the word of truth.
²Tim 2:15

Date:
Speaker:
Sermon Title:

Scripture Notes

Personal Revelation:

Appointments:

Tithe/Offering:

LUKE

Study to show thyself approved unto God,
A workman that needeth not be ashamed
rightly dividing the word of truth.
²Tim 2:15

Date:
Speaker:
Sermon Title:

Scripture Notes

LUKE

Personal Revelation:

Appointments:

Tithe/Offering:

Study to show thyself approved unto God,
A workman that needeth not be ashamed
rightly dividing the word of truth.
²Tim 2:15

Date:
Speaker:
Sermon Title:

Scripture Notes

Personal Revelation:

Appointments:

Tithe/Offering:

LUKE

Study to show thyself approved unto God,
A workman that needeth not be ashamed
rightly dividing the word of truth.
2Tim 2:15

Date:
Speaker:
Sermon Title:

Scripture Notes

Personal Revelation:

Appointments:

Tithe/Offering:

LUKE

Study to show thyself approved unto God,
A workman that needeth not be ashamed
rightly dividing the word of truth.
²Tim 2:15

Date:
Speaker:
Sermon Title:

Scripture Notes

LUKE

Personal Revelation:

Appointments:

Tithe/Offering:

Study to show thyself approved unto God,
A workman that needeth not be ashamed
rightly dividing the word of truth.
²Tim 2:15

Date:

Speaker:

Sermon Title:

Scripture Notes

Personal Revelation:

Appointments:

Tithe/Offering:

LUKE

Study to show thyself approved unto God,
A workman that needeth not be ashamed
rightly dividing the word of truth.
²Tim 2:15

Date:
Speaker:
Sermon Title:

Scripture Notes

Personal Revelation:

Appointments:

Tithe/Offering:

JOHN

Study to show thyself approved unto God,
A workman that needeth not be ashamed
rightly dividing the word of truth.
²Tim 2:15

Date:
Speaker:
Sermon Title:

Scripture Notes

Personal Revelation:

Appointments:

Tithe/Offering:

JOHN

Study to show thyself approved unto God,
A workman that needeth not be ashamed
rightly dividing the word of truth.
²Tim 2:15

Date:
Speaker:
Sermon Title:

Scripture Notes

JOHN

Personal Revelation:

Appointments:

Tithe/Offering:

Study to show thyself approved unto God,
A workman that needeth not be ashamed
rightly dividing the word of truth.
²Tim 2:15

Date:

Speaker:

Sermon Title:

Scripture Notes

JOHN

Personal Revelation:

Appointments:

Tithe/Offering:

Study to show thyself approved unto God,
A workman that needeth not be ashamed
rightly dividing the word of truth.
²Tim 2:15

Date:
Speaker:
Sermon Title:

Scripture Notes

JOHN

Personal Revelation:

Appointments:

Tithe/Offering:

Study to show thyself approved unto God,
A workman that needeth not be ashamed
rightly dividing the word of truth.
²Tim 2:15

Date:
Speaker:
Sermon Title:

Scripture Notes

Personal Revelation:

Appointments:

Tithe/Offering:

JOHN

Study to show thyself approved unto God,
A workman that needeth not be ashamed
rightly dividing the word of truth.
²Tim 2:15

Date:
Speaker:
Sermon Title:

Scripture Notes

JOHN

Personal Revelation:

Appointments:

Tithe/Offering:

Study to show thyself approved unto God,
A workman that needeth not be ashamed
rightly dividing the word of truth.
²Tim 2:15

Date:
Speaker:
Sermon Title:

Scripture Notes

ACTS

Personal Revelation:

Appointments:

Tithe/Offering:

Study to show thyself approved unto God,
A workman that needeth not be ashamed
rightly dividing the word of truth.
²Tim 2:15

Date:
Speaker:
Sermon Title:

Scripture Notes

Personal Revelation:

Appointments:

Tithe/Offering:

ACTS

> *Study to show thyself approved unto God,*
> *A workman that needeth not be ashamed*
> *rightly dividing the word of truth.*
> *²Tim 2:15*

Date:

Speaker:

Sermon Title:

Scripture Notes

ACTS

Personal Revelation:

Appointments:

Tithe/Offering:

Study to show thyself approved unto God,
A workman that needeth not be ashamed
rightly dividing the word of truth.
²Tim 2:15

Date:
Speaker:
Sermon Title:

Scripture Notes

ACTS

Personal Revelation:

Appointments:

Tithe/Offering:

Study to show thyself approved unto God,
A workman that needeth not be ashamed
rightly dividing the word of truth.
²Tim 2:15

Date:

Speaker:

Sermon Title:

Scripture Notes

Personal Revelation:

Appointments:

Tithe/Offering:

ACTS

Darcell Lemmons

Study to show thyself approved unto God,
A workman that needeth not be ashamed
rightly dividing the word of truth.
²Tim 2:15

Date:
Speaker:
Sermon Title:

Scripture Notes

ACTS

Personal Revelation:

Appointments:

Tithe/Offering:

318

Study to show thyself approved unto God,
A workman that needeth not be ashamed
rightly dividing the word of truth.
²Tim 2:15

Date:

Speaker:

Sermon Title:

Scripture Notes

Personal Revelation:

Appointments:

Tithe/Offering:

ACTS

Study to show thyself approved unto God,
A workman that needeth not be ashamed
rightly dividing the word of truth.
²Tim 2:15

Date:

Speaker:

Sermon Title:

Scripture Notes

Personal Revelation:

Appointments:

Tithe/Offering:

ROMANS

Study to show thyself approved unto God,
A workman that needeth not be ashamed
rightly dividing the word of truth.
²Tim 2:15

Date:
Speaker:
Sermon Title:

Scripture Notes

ROMANS

Personal Revelation:

Appointments:

Tithe/Offering:

Study to show thyself approved unto God,
A workman that needeth not be ashamed
rightly dividing the word of truth.
²Tim 2:15

Date:
Speaker:
Sermon Title:

Scripture Notes

ROMANS

Personal Revelation:

Appointments:

Tithe/Offering:

Study to show thyself approved unto God,
A workman that needeth not be ashamed
rightly dividing the word of truth.
²Tim 2:15

Date:
Speaker:
Sermon Title:

Scripture Notes

ROMANS

Personal Revelation:

Appointments:

Tithe/Offering:

Study to show thyself approved unto God,
A workman that needeth not be ashamed
rightly dividing the word of truth.
²Tim 2:15

Date:
Speaker:
Sermon Title:

Scripture Notes

Personal Revelation:

Appointments:

Tithe/Offering:

ROMANS

Study to show thyself approved unto God,
A workman that needeth not be ashamed
rightly dividing the word of truth.
²Tim 2:15

Date:
Speaker:
Sermon Title:

Scripture Notes

Personal Revelation:

Appointments:

Tithe/Offering:

ROMANS

Study to show thyself approved unto God,
A workman that needeth not be ashamed
rightly dividing the word of truth.
²Tim 2:15

Date:
Speaker:
Sermon Title:

Scripture Notes

Personal Revelation:

Appointments:

Tithe/Offering:

ROMANS

Study to show thyself approved unto God,
A workman that needeth not be ashamed
rightly dividing the word of truth.
²Tim 2:15

Date:
Speaker:
Sermon Title:

Scripture Notes

Personal Revelation:

Appointments:

Tithe/Offering:

1CORINTHIANS

Study to show thyself approved unto God,
A workman that needeth not be ashamed
rightly dividing the word of truth.
²Tim 2:15

Date:
Speaker:
Sermon Title:

Scripture Notes

Personal Revelation:

Appointments:

Tithe/Offering:

1CORINTHIANS

Study to show thyself approved unto God,
A workman that needeth not be ashamed
rightly dividing the word of truth.
²Tim 2:15

Date:
Speaker:
Sermon Title:

Scripture Notes

Personal Revelation:

Appointments:

Tithe/Offering:

1CORINTHIANS

Study to show thyself approved unto God,
A workman that needeth not be ashamed
rightly dividing the word of truth.
²Tim 2:15

Date:
Speaker:
Sermon Title:

Scripture Notes

Personal Revelation:

Appointments:

Tithe/Offering:

1CORINTHIANS

Study to show thyself approved unto God,
A workman that needeth not be ashamed
rightly dividing the word of truth.
²Tim 2:15

Date:

Speaker:

Sermon Title:

Scripture Notes

Personal Revelation:

Appointments:

Tithe/Offering:

1CORINTHIANS

> *Study to show thyself approved unto God,*
> *A workman that needeth not be ashamed*
> *rightly dividing the word of truth.*
> *²Tim 2:15*

Date:

Speaker:

Sermon Title:

Scripture Notes

Personal Revelation:

Appointments:

Tithe/Offering:

1CORINTHIANS

Study to show thyself approved unto God,
A workman that needeth not be ashamed
rightly dividing the word of truth.
2Tim 2:15

Date:
Speaker:
Sermon Title:

Scripture Notes

Personal Revelation:

Appointments:

Tithe/Offering:

1CORINTHIANS

Study to show thyself approved unto God,
A workman that needeth not be ashamed
rightly dividing the word of truth.
²Tim 2:15

Date:

Speaker:

Sermon Title:

Scripture Notes

Personal Revelation:

Appointments:

Tithe/Offering:

²CORINTHIANS

Study to show thyself approved unto God,
A workman that needeth not be ashamed
rightly dividing the word of truth.
²Tim 2:15

Date:
Speaker:
Sermon Title:

Scripture Notes

Personal Revelation:

Appointments:

Tithe/Offering:

²CORINTHIANS

Darcell Lemmons

Study to show thyself approved unto God,
A workman that needeth not be ashamed
rightly dividing the word of truth.
²Tim 2:15

Date:
Speaker:
Sermon Title:

Scripture Notes

²CORINTHIANS

Personal Revelation:

Appointments:

Tithe/Offering:

Study to show thyself approved unto God,
A workman that needeth not be ashamed
rightly dividing the word of truth.
²Tim 2:15

Date:

Speaker:

Sermon Title:

Scripture Notes

2CORINTHIANS

Personal Revelation:

Appointments:

Tithe/Offering:

Study to show thyself approved unto God,
A workman that needeth not be ashamed
rightly dividing the word of truth.
²Tim 2:15

Date:

Speaker:

Sermon Title:

Scripture Notes

Personal Revelation:

Appointments:

Tithe/Offering:

²CORINTHIANS

Study to show thyself approved unto God,
A workman that needeth not be ashamed
rightly dividing the word of truth.
²Tim 2:15

Date:

Speaker:

Sermon Title:

Scripture Notes

Personal Revelation:

Appointments:

Tithe/Offering:

2CORINTHIANS

> *Study to show thyself approved unto God,*
> *A workman that needeth not be ashamed*
> *rightly dividing the word of truth.*
> *²Tim 2:15*

Date:
Speaker:
Sermon Title:

Scripture Notes

Personal Revelation:

Appointments:

Tithe/Offering:

2CORINTHIANS

Study to show thyself approved unto God,
A workman that needeth not be ashamed
rightly dividing the word of truth.
²Tim 2:15

Date:
Speaker:
Sermon Title:

Scripture Notes

Personal Revelation:

Appointments:

Tithe/Offering:

GALATIANS

Study to show thyself approved unto God, A workman that needeth not be ashamed rightly dividing the word of truth.   *²Tim 2:15*
Date:
Speaker:
Sermon Title:
Scripture Notes
Personal Revelation:
Appointments:
Tithe/Offering:

GALATIANS

Study to show thyself approved unto God,
A workman that needeth not be ashamed
rightly dividing the word of truth.
²Tim 2:15

Date:

Speaker:

Sermon Title:

Scripture Notes

GALATIANS

Personal Revelation:

Appointments:

Tithe/Offering:

Darcell Lemmons

***Study to show thyself approved unto God,
A workman that needeth not be ashamed
rightly dividing the word of truth.***
²Tim 2:15

Date:
Speaker:
Sermon Title:
Scripture Notes

Personal Revelation:

Appointments:

Tithe/Offering:

GALATIANS

Study to show thyself approved unto God,
A workman that needeth not be ashamed
rightly dividing the word of truth.
²Tim 2:15

Date:
Speaker:
Sermon Title:

Scripture Notes

Personal Revelation:

Appointments:

Tithe/Offering:

GALATIANS

Study to show thyself approved unto God,
A workman that needeth not be ashamed
rightly dividing the word of truth.
²Tim 2:15

Date:
Speaker:
Sermon Title:

Scripture Notes

Personal Revelation:

Appointments:

Tithe/Offering:

GALATIANS

Study to show thyself approved unto God,
A workman that needeth not be ashamed
rightly dividing the word of truth.
²Tim 2:15

Date:
Speaker:
Sermon Title:

Scripture Notes

Personal Revelation:

Appointments:

Tithe/Offering:

GALATIANS

Darcell Lemmons

Study to show thyself approved unto God,
A workman that needeth not be ashamed
rightly dividing the word of truth.
²Tim 2:15

Date:
Speaker:
Sermon Title:

Scripture Notes

Personal Revelation:

Appointments:

Tithe/Offering:

EPHESIANS

Study to show thyself approved unto God,
A workman that needeth not be ashamed
rightly dividing the word of truth.
²Tim 2:15

Date:
Speaker:
Sermon Title:

Scripture Notes

Personal Revelation:

Appointments:

Tithe/Offering:

EPHESIANS

Study to show thyself approved unto God,
A workman that needeth not be ashamed
rightly dividing the word of truth.
²Tim 2:15

Date:
Speaker:
Sermon Title:

Scripture Notes

Personal Revelation:

Appointments:

Tithe/Offering:

EPHESIANS

Study to show thyself approved unto God,
A workman that needeth not be ashamed
rightly dividing the word of truth.
²Tim 2:15

Date:
Speaker:
Sermon Title:

Scripture Notes

Personal Revelation:

Appointments:

Tithe/Offering:

EPHESIANS

> ***Study to show thyself approved unto God,***
> ***A workman that needeth not be ashamed***
> ***rightly dividing the word of truth.***
> ***²Tim 2:15***

Date:

Speaker:

Sermon Title:

Scripture Notes

Personal Revelation:

Appointments:

Tithe/Offering:

EPHESIANS

Study to show thyself approved unto God,
A workman that needeth not be ashamed
rightly dividing the word of truth.
²Tim 2:15

Date:

Speaker:

Sermon Title:

Scripture Notes

Personal Revelation:

Appointments:

Tithe/Offering:

EPHESIANS

Study to show thyself approved unto God,
A workman that needeth not be ashamed
rightly dividing the word of truth.
²Tim 2:15

Date:
Speaker:
Sermon Title:

Scripture Notes

Personal Revelation:

Appointments:

Tithe/Offering:

EPHESIANS

Study to show thyself approved unto God,
A workman that needeth not be ashamed
rightly dividing the word of truth.
²Tim 2:15

Date:
Speaker:
Sermon Title:

Scripture Notes

Personal Revelation:

Appointments:

Tithe/Offering:

PHILIPPIANS

Study to show thyself approved unto God,
A workman that needeth not be ashamed
rightly dividing the word of truth.
²Tim 2:15

Date:
Speaker:
Sermon Title:

Scripture Notes

PHILIPPIANS

Personal Revelation:

Appointments:

Tithe/Offering:

Study to show thyself approved unto God,
A workman that needeth not be ashamed
rightly dividing the word of truth.
²Tim 2:15

Date:
Speaker:
Sermon Title:

Scripture Notes

Personal Revelation:

Appointments:

Tithe/Offering:

PHILIPPIANS

Study to show thyself approved unto God,
A workman that needeth not be ashamed
rightly dividing the word of truth.
²Tim 2:15

Date:

Speaker:

Sermon Title:

Scripture Notes

Personal Revelation:

Appointments:

Tithe/Offering:

PHILIPPIANS

Study to show thyself approved unto God,
A workman that needeth not be ashamed
rightly dividing the word of truth.
²Tim 2:15

Date:
Speaker:
Sermon Title:

Scripture Notes

Personal Revelation:

Appointments:

Tithe/Offering:

PHILIPPIANS

Study to show thyself approved unto God,
A workman that needeth not be ashamed
rightly dividing the word of truth.
²Tim 2:15

Date:
Speaker:
Sermon Title:

Scripture Notes

PHILIPPIANS

Personal Revelation:

Appointments:

Tithe/Offering:

Study to show thyself approved unto God,
A workman that needeth not be ashamed
rightly dividing the word of truth.
²Tim 2:15

Date:
Speaker:
Sermon Title:

Scripture Notes

Personal Revelation:

Appointments:

Tithe/Offering:

PHILIPPIANS

Study to show thyself approved unto God,
A workman that needeth not be ashamed
rightly dividing the word of truth.
²Tim 2:15

Date:
Speaker:
Sermon Title:

Scripture Notes

Personal Revelation:

Appointments:

Tithe/Offering:

COLOSSIANS

Study to show thyself approved unto God,
A workman that needeth not be ashamed
rightly dividing the word of truth.
²Tim 2:15

Date:
Speaker:
Sermon Title:

Scripture Notes

Personal Revelation:

Appointments:

Tithe/Offering:

COLOSSIANS

Darcell Lemmons

> *Study to show thyself approved unto God,*
> *A workman that needeth not be ashamed*
> *rightly dividing the word of truth.*
> *²Tim 2:15*

Date:
Speaker:
Sermon Title:

Scripture Notes

Personal Revelation:

Appointments:

Tithe/Offering:

COLOSSIANS

Study to show thyself approved unto God,
A workman that needeth not be ashamed
rightly dividing the word of truth.
²Tim 2:15

Date:

Speaker:

Sermon Title:

Scripture Notes

Personal Revelation:

Appointments:

Tithe/Offering:

COLOSSIANS

Study to show thyself approved unto God,
A workman that needeth not be ashamed
rightly dividing the word of truth.
²Tim 2:15

Date:
Speaker:
Sermon Title:

Scripture Notes

Personal Revelation:

Appointments:

Tithe/Offering:

COLOSSIANS

Study to show thyself approved unto God,
A workman that needeth not be ashamed
rightly dividing the word of truth.
²Tim 2:15

Date:
Speaker:
Sermon Title:

Scripture Notes

Personal Revelation:

Appointments:

Tithe/Offering:

COLOSSIANS

Study to show thyself approved unto God,
A workman that needeth not be ashamed
rightly dividing the word of truth.
²Tim 2:15

Date:
Speaker:
Sermon Title:

Scripture Notes

Personal Revelation:

Appointments:

Tithe/Offering:

COLOSSIANS

Study to show thyself approved unto God,
A workman that needeth not be ashamed
rightly dividing the word of truth.
²Tim 2:15

Date:

Speaker:

Sermon Title:

Scripture Notes

Personal Revelation:

Appointments:

Tithe/Offering:

1THESSALONIANS

Study to show thyself approved unto God,
A workman that needeth not be ashamed
rightly dividing the word of truth.
²Tim 2:15

Date:
Speaker:
Sermon Title:

Scripture Notes

Personal Revelation:

Appointments:

Tithe/Offering:

1THESSALONIANS

Study to show thyself approved unto God,
A workman that needeth not be ashamed
rightly dividing the word of truth.
²Tim 2:15

Date:
Speaker:
Sermon Title:

Scripture Notes

Personal Revelation:

Appointments:

Tithe/Offering:

¹THESSALONIANS

> *Study to show thyself approved unto God,*
> *A workman that needeth not be ashamed*
> *rightly dividing the word of truth.*
> *²Tim 2:15*

Date:
Speaker:
Sermon Title:

Scripture Notes

Personal Revelation:

Appointments:

Tithe/Offering:

1THESSALONIANS

Study to show thyself approved unto God,
A workman that needeth not be ashamed
rightly dividing the word of truth.
²Tim 2:15

Date:

Speaker:

Sermon Title:

Scripture Notes

Personal Revelation:

Appointments:

Tithe/Offering:

1THESSALONIANS

Study to show thyself approved unto God,
A workman that needeth not be ashamed
rightly dividing the word of truth.
²Tim 2:15

Date:
Speaker:
Sermon Title:

Scripture Notes

1THESSALONIANS

Personal Revelation:

Appointments:

Tithe/Offering:

Study to show thyself approved unto God,
A workman that needeth not be ashamed
rightly dividing the word of truth.
²Tim 2:15

Date:
Speaker:
Sermon Title:

Scripture Notes

Personal Revelation:

Appointments:

Tithe/Offering:

1THESSALONIANS

Study to show thyself approved unto God,
A workman that needeth not be ashamed
rightly dividing the word of truth.
²Tim 2:15

Date:
Speaker:
Sermon Title:

Scripture Notes

Personal Revelation:

Appointments:

Tithe/Offering:

2THESSALONIANS

Study to show thyself approved unto God,
A workman that needeth not be ashamed
rightly dividing the word of truth.
²Tim 2:15

Date:

Speaker:

Sermon Title:

Scripture Notes

Personal Revelation:

Appointments:

Tithe/Offering:

2THESSALONIANS

Study to show thyself approved unto God,
A workman that needeth not be ashamed
rightly dividing the word of truth.
²Tim 2:15

Date:

Speaker:

Sermon Title:

Scripture Notes

Personal Revelation:

Appointments:

Tithe/Offering:

2THESSALONIANS

Study to show thyself approved unto God,
A workman that needeth not be ashamed
rightly dividing the word of truth.
²Tim 2:15

Date:
Speaker:
Sermon Title:

Scripture Notes

2THESSALONIANS

Personal Revelation:

Appointments:

Tithe/Offering:

Study to show thyself approved unto God,
A workman that needeth not be ashamed
rightly dividing the word of truth.
²Tim 2:15

Date:
Speaker:
Sermon Title:

Scripture Notes

2THESSALONIANS

Personal Revelation:

Appointments:

Tithe/Offering:

Study to show thyself approved unto God,
A workman that needeth not be ashamed
rightly dividing the word of truth.
²Tim 2:15

Date:
Speaker:
Sermon Title:

Scripture Notes

Personal Revelation:

Appointments:

Tithe/Offering:

2THESSALONIANS

Study to show thyself approved unto God,
A workman that needeth not be ashamed
rightly dividing the word of truth.
²Tim 2:15

Date:

Speaker:

Sermon Title:

Scripture Notes

2THESSALONIANS

Personal Revelation:

Appointments:

Tithe/Offering:

Study to show thyself approved unto God,
A workman that needeth not be ashamed
rightly dividing the word of truth.
²Tim 2:15

Date:
Speaker:
Sermon Title:

Scripture Notes

Personal Revelation:

Appointments:

Tithe/Offering:

1TIMOTHY

Study to show thyself approved unto God,
A workman that needeth not be ashamed
rightly dividing the word of truth.
²Tim 2:15

Date:

Speaker:

Sermon Title:

Scripture Notes

1TIMOTHY

Personal Revelation:

Appointments:

Tithe/Offering:

Study to show thyself approved unto God,
A workman that needeth not be ashamed
rightly dividing the word of truth.
²Tim 2:15

Date:
Speaker:
Sermon Title:

Scripture Notes

1TIMOTHY

Personal Revelation:

Appointments:

Tithe/Offering:

> *Study to show thyself approved unto God,*
> *A workman that needeth not be ashamed*
> *rightly dividing the word of truth.*
> *²Tim 2:15*

Date:

Speaker:

Sermon Title:

Scripture Notes

¹TIMOTHY

Personal Revelation:

Appointments:

Tithe/Offering:

Study to show thyself approved unto God,
A workman that needeth not be ashamed
rightly dividing the word of truth.
²Tim 2:15

Date:
Speaker:
Sermon Title:

Scripture Notes

1TIMOTHY

Personal Revelation:

Appointments:

Tithe/Offering:

*Study to show thyself approved unto God,
A workman that needeth not be ashamed
rightly dividing the word of truth.*
²Tim 2:15

Date:
Speaker:
Sermon Title:

Scripture Notes

¹TIMOTHY

Personal Revelation:

Appointments:

Tithe/Offering:

Study to show thyself approved unto God,
A workman that needeth not be ashamed
rightly dividing the word of truth.
²Tim 2:15

Date:
Speaker:
Sermon Title:

Scripture Notes

Personal Revelation:

Appointments:

Tithe/Offering:

¹TIMOTHY

> *Study to show thyself approved unto God,*
> *A workman that needeth not be ashamed*
> *rightly dividing the word of truth.*
> *²Tim 2:15*

Date:

Speaker:

Sermon Title:

Scripture Notes

Personal Revelation:

Appointments:

Tithe/Offering:

2TIMOTHY

Study to show thyself approved unto God,
A workman that needeth not be ashamed
rightly dividing the word of truth.
²Tim 2:15

Date:
Speaker:
Sermon Title:

Scripture Notes

Personal Revelation:

Appointments:

Tithe/Offering:

2TIMOTHY

Study to show thyself approved unto God,
A workman that needeth not be ashamed
rightly dividing the word of truth.
²Tim 2:15

Date:
Speaker:
Sermon Title:

Scripture Notes

Personal Revelation:

Appointments:

Tithe/Offering:

2TIMOTHY

Study to show thyself approved unto God,
A workman that needeth not be ashamed
rightly dividing the word of truth.
²Tim 2:15

Date:
Speaker:
Sermon Title:

Scripture Notes

Personal Revelation:

Appointments:

Tithe/Offering:

2TIMOTHY

Study to show thyself approved unto God,
A workman that needeth not be ashamed
rightly dividing the word of truth.
²Tim 2:15

Date:

Speaker:

Sermon Title:

Scripture Notes

Personal Revelation:

Appointments:

Tithe/Offering:

2TIMOTHY

> *Study to show thyself approved unto God,*
> *A workman that needeth not be ashamed*
> *rightly dividing the word of truth.*
> *²Tim 2:15*

Date:
Speaker:
Sermon Title:

Scripture Notes

2TIMOTHY

Personal Revelation:

Appointments:

Tithe/Offering:

> *Study to show thyself approved unto God,*
> *A workman that needeth not be ashamed*
> *rightly dividing the word of truth.*
> *²Tim 2:15*

Date:
Speaker:
Sermon Title:

Scripture Notes

2TIMOTHY

Personal Revelation:

Appointments:

Tithe/Offering:

Study to show thyself approved unto God, A workman that needeth not be ashamed rightly dividing the word of truth.
²Tim 2:15

Date:
Speaker:
Sermon Title:

Scripture Notes

Personal Revelation:

Appointments:

Tithe/Offering:

TITUS

> ***Study to show thyself approved unto God, A workman that needeth not be ashamed rightly dividing the word of truth.***
> ***²Tim 2:15***

Date:
Speaker:
Sermon Title:

Scripture Notes

TITUS

Personal Revelation:

Appointments:

Tithe/Offering:

Study to show thyself approved unto God, A workman that needeth not be ashamed rightly dividing the word of truth.
²Tim 2:15

Date:
Speaker:
Sermon Title:

Scripture Notes

Personal Revelation:

Appointments:

Tithe/Offering:

TITUS

> ***Study to show thyself approved unto God, A workman that needeth not be ashamed rightly dividing the word of truth.***
> *²Tim 2:15*

Date:
Speaker:
Sermon Title:

Scripture Notes

TITUS

Personal Revelation:

Appointments:

Tithe/Offering:

Study to show thyself approved unto God, A workman that needeth not be ashamed rightly dividing the word of truth.
²Tim 2:15

Date:
Speaker:
Sermon Title:

Scripture Notes

Personal Revelation:

Appointments:

Tithe/Offering:

TITUS

Study to show thyself approved unto God, A workman that needeth not be ashamed rightly dividing the word of truth.
²Tim 2:15

Date:
Speaker:
Sermon Title:

Scripture Notes

Personal Revelation:

Appointments:

Tithe/Offering:

TITUS

Study to show thyself approved unto God, A workman that needeth not be ashamed rightly dividing the word of truth.
²Tim 2:15

Date:
Speaker:
Sermon Title:

Scripture Notes

Personal Revelation:

Appointments:

Tithe/Offering:

TITUS

Study to show thyself approved unto God, A workman that needeth not be ashamed rightly dividing the word of truth.
²Tim 2:15

Date:
Speaker:
Sermon Title:

Scripture Notes

Personal Revelation:

Appointments:

Tithe/Offering:

PHILEMON

Study to show thyself approved unto God, A workman that needeth not be ashamed rightly dividing the word of truth.
²Tim 2:15

Date:
Speaker:
Sermon Title:

Scripture Notes

Personal Revelation:

Appointments:

Tithe/Offering:

PHILEMON

Study to show thyself approved unto God, A workman that needeth not be ashamed rightly dividing the word of truth.
²Tim 2:15

Date:
Speaker:
Sermon Title:

Scripture Notes

PHILEMON

Personal Revelation:

Appointments:

Tithe/Offering:

Study to show thyself approved unto God, A workman that needeth not be ashamed rightly dividing the word of truth.
²Tim 2:15

Date:
Speaker:
Sermon Title:

Scripture Notes

PHILEMON

Personal Revelation:

Appointments:

Tithe/Offering:

Study to show thyself approved unto God, A workman that needeth not be ashamed rightly dividing the word of truth.
²Tim 2:15

Date:
Speaker:
Sermon Title:

Scripture Notes

PHILEMON

Personal Revelation:

Appointments:

Tithe/Offering:

Study to show thyself approved unto God, A workman that needeth not be ashamed rightly dividing the word of truth.
²Tim 2:15

Date:
Speaker:
Sermon Title:

Scripture Notes

Personal Revelation:

Appointments:

Tithe/Offering:

PHILEMON

Study to show thyself approved unto God, A workman that needeth not be ashamed rightly dividing the word of truth. *²Tim 2:15*	
Date: **Speaker:** **Sermon Title:**	**PHILEMON**
Scripture Notes	

Personal Revelation:

Appointments:

Tithe/Offering:

Study to show thyself approved unto God, A workman that needeth not be ashamed rightly dividing the word of truth.
²Tim 2:15

Date:
Speaker:
Sermon Title:

Scripture Notes

HEBREWS

Personal Revelation:

Appointments:

Tithe/Offering:

> ***Study to show thyself approved unto God, A workman that needeth not be ashamed rightly dividing the word of truth.***
> ***²Tim 2:15***

Date:
Speaker:
Sermon Title:

Scripture Notes

HEBREWS

Personal Revelation:

Appointments:

Tithe/Offering:

Study to show thyself approved unto God, A workman that needeth not be ashamed rightly dividing the word of truth.
²Tim 2:15

Date:
Speaker:
Sermon Title:

Scripture Notes

HEBREWS

Personal Revelation:

Appointments:

Tithe/Offering:

> ***Study to show thyself approved unto God, A workman that needeth not be ashamed rightly dividing the word of truth.***
> ***²Tim 2:15***

Date:

Speaker:

Sermon Title:

Scripture Notes

Personal Revelation:

Appointments:

Tithe/Offering:

HEBREWS

Study to show thyself approved unto God, A workman that needeth not be ashamed rightly dividing the word of truth.
²Tim 2:15

Date:
Speaker:
Sermon Title:

Scripture Notes

Personal Revelation:

Appointments:

Tithe/Offering:

HEBREWS

> ***Study to show thyself approved unto God, A workman that needeth not be ashamed rightly dividing the word of truth.***
> ***²Tim 2:15***

Date:
Speaker:
Sermon Title:

Scripture Notes

HEBREWS

Personal Revelation:

Appointments:

Tithe/Offering:

Study to show thyself approved unto God, A workman that needeth not be ashamed rightly dividing the word of truth.
²Tim 2:15

Date:
Speaker:
Sermon Title:

Scripture Notes

Personal Revelation:

Appointments:

Tithe/Offering:

HEBREWS

Study to show thyself approved unto God, A workman that needeth not be ashamed rightly dividing the word of truth.
²Tim 2:15

Date:
Speaker:
Sermon Title:

Scripture Notes

JAMES

Personal Revelation:

Appointments:

Tithe/Offering:

Study to show thyself approved unto God, A workman that needeth not be ashamed rightly dividing the word of truth.
²Tim 2:15

Date:
Speaker:
Sermon Title:

Scripture Notes

Personal Revelation:

Appointments:

Tithe/Offering:

JAMES

> ***Study to show thyself approved unto God, A workman that needeth not be ashamed rightly dividing the word of truth.***
> ***²Tim 2:15***

Date:

Speaker:

Sermon Title:

Scripture Notes

JAMES

Personal Revelation:

Appointments:

Tithe/Offering:

Study to show thyself approved unto God, A workman that needeth not be ashamed rightly dividing the word of truth.
²Tim 2:15

Date:
Speaker:
Sermon Title:

Scripture Notes

JAMES

Personal Revelation:

Appointments:

Tithe/Offering:

> ***Study to show thyself approved unto God, A workman that needeth not be ashamed rightly dividing the word of truth.***
> *²Tim 2:15*

Date:
Speaker:
Sermon Title:

Scripture Notes

JAMES

Personal Revelation:

Appointments:

Tithe/Offering:

Study to show thyself approved unto God, A workman that needeth not be ashamed rightly dividing the word of truth.
²Tim 2:15

Date:
Speaker:
Sermon Title:

Scripture Notes

Personal Revelation:

Appointments:

Tithe/Offering:

JAMES

Study to show thyself approved unto God, A workman that needeth not be ashamed rightly dividing the word of truth.
²Tim 2:15

Date:
Speaker:
Sermon Title:

Scripture Notes

Personal Revelation:

Appointments:

Tithe/Offering:

JAMES

Study to show thyself approved unto God,
A workman that needeth not be ashamed
rightly dividing the word of truth.
2Tim 2:15

Date:
Speaker:
Sermon Title:

Scripture Notes

Personal Revelation:

Appointments:

Tithe/Offering:

1PETER

Study to show thyself approved unto God,
A workman that needeth not be ashamed
rightly dividing the word of truth.
²Tim 2:15

Date:

Speaker:

Sermon Title:

Scripture Notes

Personal Revelation:

Appointments:

Tithe/Offering:

1PETER

> *Study to show thyself approved unto God,*
> *A workman that needeth not be ashamed*
> *rightly dividing the word of truth.*
> *²Tim 2:15*

Date:
Speaker:
Sermon Title:

Scripture Notes

1PETER

Personal Revelation:

Appointments:

Tithe/Offering:

Darcell Lemmons

Study to show thyself approved unto God,
A workman that needeth not be ashamed
rightly dividing the word of truth.
²Tim 2:15

Date:
Speaker:
Sermon Title:

Scripture Notes

1PETER

Personal Revelation:

Appointments:

Tithe/Offering:

Study to show thyself approved unto God,
A workman that needeth not be ashamed
rightly dividing the word of truth.
²Tim 2:15

Date:

Speaker:

Sermon Title:

Scripture Notes

1PETER

Personal Revelation:

Appointments:

Tithe/Offering:

Study to show thyself approved unto God,
A workman that needeth not be ashamed
rightly dividing the word of truth.
²Tim 2:15

Date:
Speaker:
Sermon Title:

Scripture Notes

1PETER

Personal Revelation:

Appointments:

Tithe/Offering:

Study to show thyself approved unto God,
A workman that needeth not be ashamed
rightly dividing the word of truth.
²Tim 2:15

Date:

Speaker:

Sermon Title:

Scripture Notes

1PETER

Personal Revelation:

Appointments:

Tithe/Offering:

Darcell Lemmons

Study to show thyself approved unto God,
A workman that needeth not be ashamed
rightly dividing the word of truth.
²Tim 2:15

Date:
Speaker:
Sermon Title:

Scripture Notes

Personal Revelation:

Appointments:

Tithe/Offering:

2PETER

Study to show thyself approved unto God,
A workman that needeth not be ashamed
rightly dividing the word of truth.
²Tim 2:15

Date:
Speaker:
Sermon Title:

Scripture Notes

Personal Revelation:

Appointments:

Tithe/Offering:

2PETER

Study to show thyself approved unto God,
A workman that needeth not be ashamed
rightly dividing the word of truth.
²Tim 2:15

Date:
Speaker:
Sermon Title:

Scripture Notes

Personal Revelation:

Appointments:

Tithe/Offering:

²PETER

Study to show thyself approved unto God,
A workman that needeth not be ashamed
rightly dividing the word of truth.
²Tim 2:15

Date:
Speaker:
Sermon Title:

Scripture Notes

²PETER

Personal Revelation:

Appointments:

Tithe/Offering:

Study to show thyself approved unto God,
A workman that needeth not be ashamed
rightly dividing the word of truth.
²Tim 2:15

Date:
Speaker:
Sermon Title:

Scripture Notes

2PETER

Personal Revelation:

Appointments:

Tithe/Offering:

Study to show thyself approved unto God,
A workman that needeth not be ashamed
rightly dividing the word of truth.
²Tim 2:15

Date:
Speaker:
Sermon Title:

Scripture Notes

2 PETER

Personal Revelation:

Appointments:

Tithe/Offering:

> *Study to show thyself approved unto God,*
> *A workman that needeth not be ashamed*
> *rightly dividing the word of truth.*
> *²Tim 2:15*

Date:
Speaker:
Sermon Title:

Scripture Notes

Personal Revelation:

Appointments:

Tithe/Offering:

²PETER

Study to show thyself approved unto God,
A workman that needeth not be ashamed
rightly dividing the word of truth.
²Tim 2:15

Date:
Speaker:
Sermon Title:

Scripture Notes

Personal Revelation:

Appointments:

Tithe/Offering:

1JOHN

Study to show thyself approved unto God,
A workman that needeth not be ashamed
rightly dividing the word of truth.
²Tim 2:15

Date:

Speaker:

Sermon Title:

Scripture Notes

Personal Revelation:

Appointments:

Tithe/Offering:

1 JOHN

Study to show thyself approved unto God,
A workman that needeth not be ashamed
rightly dividing the word of truth.
²Tim 2:15

Date:
Speaker:
Sermon Title:

Scripture Notes

1JOHN

Personal Revelation:

Appointments:

Tithe/Offering:

Darcell Lemmons

> *Study to show thyself approved unto God,*
> *A workman that needeth not be ashamed*
> *rightly dividing the word of truth.*
> *²Tim 2:15*

Date:
Speaker:
Sermon Title:

Scripture Notes

1 JOHN

Personal Revelation:

Appointments:

Tithe/Offering:

Study to show thyself approved unto God,
A workman that needeth not be ashamed
rightly dividing the word of truth.
²Tim 2:15

Date:
Speaker:
Sermon Title:

Scripture Notes

Personal Revelation:

Appointments:

Tithe/Offering:

1 JOHN

Study to show thyself approved unto God,
A workman that needeth not be ashamed
rightly dividing the word of truth.
²Tim 2:15

Date:

Speaker:

Sermon Title:

Scripture Notes

1JOHN

Personal Revelation:

Appointments:

Tithe/Offering:

Study to show thyself approved unto God,
A workman that needeth not be ashamed
rightly dividing the word of truth.
²Tim 2:15

Date:
Speaker:
Sermon Title:

Scripture Notes

1 JOHN

Personal Revelation:

Appointments:

Tithe/Offering:

Study to show thyself approved unto God,
A workman that needeth not be ashamed
rightly dividing the word of truth.
²Tim 2:15

Date:
Speaker:
Sermon Title:

Scripture Notes

2 JOHN

Personal Revelation:

Appointments:

Tithe/Offering:

Study to show thyself approved unto God,
A workman that needeth not be ashamed
rightly dividing the word of truth.
²Tim 2:15

Date:

Speaker:

Sermon Title:

Scripture Notes

Personal Revelation:

Appointments:

Tithe/Offering:

2 JOHN

Study to show thyself approved unto God,
A workman that needeth not be ashamed
rightly dividing the word of truth.
²Tim 2:15

Date:
Speaker:
Sermon Title:

Scripture Notes

Personal Revelation:

Appointments:

Tithe/Offering:

2 JOHN

Study to show thyself approved unto God,
A workman that needeth not be ashamed
rightly dividing the word of truth.
²Tim 2:15

Date:
Speaker:
Sermon Title:

Scripture Notes

2 JOHN

Personal Revelation:

Appointments:

Tithe/Offering:

Study to show thyself approved unto God,
A workman that needeth not be ashamed
rightly dividing the word of truth.
²Tim 2:15

Date:
Speaker:
Sermon Title:

Scripture Notes

Personal Revelation:

Appointments:

Tithe/Offering:

2 JOHN

Study to show thyself approved unto God,
A workman that needeth not be ashamed
rightly dividing the word of truth.
²Tim 2:15

Date:
Speaker:
Sermon Title:

Scripture Notes

Personal Revelation:

Appointments:

Tithe/Offering:

2 JOHN

Study to show thyself approved unto God,
A workman that needeth not be ashamed
rightly dividing the word of truth.
²Tim 2:15

Date:
Speaker:
Sermon Title:

Scripture Notes

2 JOHN

Personal Revelation:

Appointments:

Tithe/Offering:

Study to show thyself approved unto God,
A workman that needeth not be ashamed
rightly dividing the word of truth.
²Tim 2:15

Date:
Speaker:
Sermon Title:

Scripture Notes

3 JOHN

Personal Revelation:

Appointments:

Tithe/Offering:

Study to show thyself approved unto God,
A workman that needeth not be ashamed
rightly dividing the word of truth.
²Tim 2:15

Date:
Speaker:
Sermon Title:

Scripture Notes

Personal Revelation:

Appointments:

Tithe/Offering:

3 JOHN

Study to show thyself approved unto God,
A workman that needeth not be ashamed
rightly dividing the word of truth.
²Tim 2:15

Date:
Speaker:
Sermon Title:

Scripture Notes

Personal Revelation:

Appointments:

Tithe/Offering:

3 JOHN

Study to show thyself approved unto God,
A workman that needeth not be ashamed
rightly dividing the word of truth.
²Tim 2:15

Date:
Speaker:
Sermon Title:

Scripture Notes

Personal Revelation:

Appointments:

Tithe/Offering:

3 JOHN

Study to show thyself approved unto God,
A workman that needeth not be ashamed
rightly dividing the word of truth.
²Tim 2:15

Date:
Speaker:
Sermon Title:

Scripture Notes

Personal Revelation:

Appointments:

Tithe/Offering:

3 JOHN

> ***Study to show thyself approved unto God,***
> ***A workman that needeth not be ashamed***
> ***rightly dividing the word of truth.***
> *²Tim 2:15*

Date:

Speaker:

Sermon Title:

Scripture Notes

Personal Revelation:

Appointments:

Tithe/Offering:

3 JOHN

*Study to show thyself approved unto God,
A workman that needeth not be ashamed
rightly dividing the word of truth.*
²Tim 2:15

Date:
Speaker:
Sermon Title:

Scripture Notes

Personal Revelation:

Appointments:

Tithe/Offering:

3 JOHN

Study to show thyself approved unto God,
A workman that needeth not be ashamed
rightly dividing the word of truth.
²Tim 2:15

Date:
Speaker:
Sermon Title:

Scripture Notes

Personal Revelation:

Appointments:

Tithe/Offering:

JUDE

Study to show thyself approved unto God,
A workman that needeth not be ashamed
rightly dividing the word of truth.
²Tim 2:15

Date:
Speaker:
Sermon Title:

Scripture Notes

Personal Revelation:

Appointments:

Tithe/Offering:

JUDE

Study to show thyself approved unto God,
A workman that needeth not be ashamed
rightly dividing the word of truth.
²Tim 2:15

Date:
Speaker:
Sermon Title:

Scripture Notes

JUDE

Personal Revelation:

Appointments:

Tithe/Offering:

Study to show thyself approved unto God,
A workman that needeth not be ashamed
rightly dividing the word of truth.
²Tim 2:15

Date:
Speaker:
Sermon Title:

Scripture Notes

JUDE

Personal Revelation:

Appointments:

Tithe/Offering:

Study to show thyself approved unto God,
A workman that needeth not be ashamed
rightly dividing the word of truth.
²Tim 2:15

Date:

Speaker:

Sermon Title:

Scripture Notes

JUDE

Personal Revelation:

Appointments:

Tithe/Offering:

Study to show thyself approved unto God,
A workman that needeth not be ashamed
rightly dividing the word of truth.
²Tim 2:15

Date:
Speaker:
Sermon Title:

Scripture Notes

JUDE

Personal Revelation:

Appointments:

Tithe/Offering:

Study to show thyself approved unto God,
A workman that needeth not be ashamed
rightly dividing the word of truth.
²Tim 2:15

Date:
Speaker:
Sermon Title:

Scripture Notes

JUDE

Personal Revelation:

Appointments:

Tithe/Offering:

Study to show thyself approved unto God,
A workman that needeth not be ashamed
rightly dividing the word of truth.
²Tim 2:15

Date:
Speaker:
Sermon Title:

Scripture Notes

Personal Revelation:

Appointments:

Tithe/Offering:

REVELATION

Study to show thyself approved unto God, A workman that needeth not be ashamed rightly dividing the word of truth.   *²Tim 2:15*

Date:
Speaker:
Sermon Title:

Scripture Notes

REVELATION

Personal Revelation:

Appointments:

Tithe/Offering:

Study to show thyself approved unto God,
A workman that needeth not be ashamed
rightly dividing the word of truth.
²Tim 2:15

Date:

Speaker:

Sermon Title:

Scripture Notes

REVELATION

Personal Revelation:

Appointments:

Tithe/Offering:

Study to show thyself approved unto God,
A workman that needeth not be ashamed
rightly dividing the word of truth.
²Tim 2:15

Date:
Speaker:
Sermon Title:

Scripture Notes

Personal Revelation:

Appointments:

Tithe/Offering:

REVELATION

Study to show thyself approved unto God,
A workman that needeth not be ashamed
rightly dividing the word of truth.
²Tim 2:15

Date:
Speaker:
Sermon Title:

Scripture Notes

Personal Revelation:

Appointments:

Tithe/Offering:

REVELATION

Study to show thyself approved unto God, A workman that needeth not be ashamed rightly dividing the word of truth.
²Tim 2:15

Date:
Speaker:
Sermon Title:

Scripture Notes

Personal Revelation:

Appointments:

Tithe/Offering:

REVELATION

Study to show thyself approved unto God,
A workman that needeth not be ashamed
rightly dividing the word of truth.
²Tim 2:15

Date:
Speaker:
Sermon Title:

Scripture Notes

Personal Revelation:

Appointments:

Tithe/Offering:

REVELATION

Golden Nuggets

A PRAYER FOR TODAY

This is the beginning of a New Day that God has given us. We can use this day to use as we will. We can waste it or use it for good, but what we do today is important because we are exchanging a day of our life for it!

When tomorrow comes, this day will be gone forever, leaving in its place something that we have traded for it.

We want it to be gain, and not loss; good and not evil; success and not failure; so that we shall not regret the price we have paid for it.

Author Unknown

Today is a gift from God, that's why we call it 'The Present'.

Psalms 68:9
Blessed be the Lord, who daily loadeth us with benefits, even the God of our salvation. Selah.

Psalms 103:2
Bless the Lord, O my soul, forget not all his benefits.

Golden Nuggets

Telephone Contacts

Name:
Address:
Ph:

Name:
Address:
Ph:

Name:
Address:
Ph:

Name:
Address:
Ph:

Name:
Address:
Ph:

Name:
Address:
Ph:

Name:
Address:
Ph:

Name:
Address:
Ph:

Telephone Contacts
Name:
Address:
Ph:
Name:
Address:
Ph:
Name:
Address:
Ph:
Name:
Address:
Ph:
Name:
Address:
Ph:
Name:
Address:
Ph:
Name:
Address:
Ph:
Name:
Address:
Ph: